The Book of Wisdom

Also by Fode Drame

The Splendors of Quran: English Translation of the Quran
Expansions Volume 1: The Purpose of Creation
Expansions Volume 2: The Way is Peace
Expansions Volume 3: The Awakening
Expansions Volume 4: The Rejuvenation of the Soul
Expansions Volume 5: The 99 Names of Allah
Expansions Volume 6: The Book of Knowledge
Illuminated Remembrance of God

Website
www.zawiyah.ca

Livestream
www.livestream.com/zawiyahfoundation

Facebook
www.facebook.com/zawiyahfoundation

Expansions
Volume 7

THE BOOK OF
WISDOM

Fode Drame

Tasleem Publications
Vancouver, BC, Canada

TASLEEM PUBLICATIONS
Expansions Volume 7: The Book of Wisdom
EXPANSIONS - VOLUME SEVEN

I. Spirituality
II. Personal Development

CONTENTS

INTRODUCTION

The word *ḥikma* (wisdom) literally means the reins by which the driver controls his mount. He pulls the reins when it goes too fast, and likewise releases them when it goes too slow. In this manner he maintains a middle pace. The term *ḥikma* is also used in a metaphorical sense to mean a body of consciousness that helps regulate the existence of an individual in a balanced fashion, touching every aspect of his life. *Ḥikma* therefore keeps the individual in check when he goes too fast and spurs him on when he is too slow. Likewise, it balances in between vertical lightness and horizontal weightiness. This is clear from the following verse:

Go forth light and heavy and strive hard with your properties and your lives in the way of Allah. That is better for you if you indeed know. (The Quran, chapter *The Repentance*, 9:41)

The Reins of the Beast

The term "*ḥikma al dāba*," the reins of the beast, consists of two parts: one pertains to the reins and the other to the beast. Each of them figuratively stands for an entity: the reins stand for wisdom since they have identical functions and the beast stands for the soul (individual self) known as *nafs* in the Arabic language. Wisdom therefore is the reins by which the ego is checked and controlled. Your soul is your beast of burden that is meant to carry you on your way to God. If you run it too fast, it will perish before you reach your destination; and if you let it linger on, you will not make it to your destination either. You must maintain a balanced and measured travel.

And We had placed between them and the cities that We blessed, other cities that were visible and We measured the journey therein. Travel in them nights and day in all safety. (The Quran, chapter *The Kingdom of Saba*, 34:18)

It is also reported that the Prophet Muhammad, peace be upon him, said: "This religion (way) is hard, therefore make your way through it gently, for one who rides his horse too fast neither covers the distance nor spares the life of his ride" (Tirmidhi).

In another prophetic tradition, he, peace be upon him, is reported to have said: "Seek help (for your journey) by morning and afternoon and the early hours of the night" (Bukhari).

You should travel by day *and* night, and during the morning *and* evening. Yet this journeying should take place only in the early and late hours of the day, as well as the early and late hours of the night. In this way you avoid becoming a perennial traveller (*al sālik al mutlaq*), and instead become a true traveller (*al sālik al mujāwib*):

> So acclaim Allah's glory when you are in the evening and when you are in the morning and for Him is the praise in the heavens and in the earth and at night and when you are in the day. (The Quran, chapter *Romans*, 30:17-18)

Wisdom entails that you apportion your time in an equitable manner between rest and action. Besides alternating between rest and action, one should also harness the force energy that nature offers by picking the right time for performing our actions: the early hours of the morning before sunrise and after sunrise or the hours of the evening before sunset and after sunset, while resting in between. Our souls get naturally charged with the energies of nature at those times.

> O you the one wrapped. Stand [for the prayer] through the night except for a little; half of it or make it a little less than that. Or make it more than that and recite the Quran with a careful recitation. (The Quran, chapter *The One Wrapped*, 73:1-4)

> Truly your Lord knows that you indeed stand [in prayer] for a little less than two thirds of the night and half of it and one third of it and so does a party of those who are with you. And Allah measures the night and the day. He knows that you will not be able to keep count of it so He turned to you in repentance therefore recite that which is easy from the Quran. He knows that there will be among you sick ones and others travelling in the earth seeking from the bounty of

Allah and others fighting in the way of Allah so recite whatever is easy thereof. So establish the prayer and offer the sanctifying dues and loan to Allah an excellent loan. And whatever good you send forth for your own souls, you will find it in Allah's presence. That is better and greater in reward. And seek forgiveness from Allah. Truly Allah is Oft-Forgiving, Most Merciful. (The Quran, chapter *The One Wrapped*, 73:20)

The Just Word

Another important detail regarding the reins and the beast is that the reins, almost exclusively, are placed in the mouth of the beast in order to control it. The mouth commonly is the means by which speech is delivered. Figuratively speaking, wisdom is the means by which we control our tongues. The lust of the tongue is one of the greatest lusts of the ego. Wisdom (the reins) keeps the tongue in check and only allows it to speak after reflection and deliberation. This makes our speech economical and impactful. The longer we keep our words back the farther they go and stronger they come out. Wisdom also enhances the value of our word, for anything that is well-kept becomes precious and anything that is vulgarized loses esteem. A wise man estimates his words to their true esteem and weighs them to their just weight. His words do full justice to the meanings they are supposed to carry and the message they are supposed to deliver. Neither in excess nor in shortage. To find the just word is the ultimate quest for those who seek wisdom. That just word is known as (*kalimatin sawā'in*).

Say, "O people of the scripture! Come unto a word which is common between us and you, that we should worship none except Allah and that we should ascribe nothing as a partner with Him and that some of us do not take others as Lords besides Allah." But if they turn away, then say, "Bear witness that we indeed are those who have submitted to Allah." (The Quran, chapter *The Family of Imran*, 3:64)

Once the just word is found, the whole being of the seeker becomes adjusted, his heart, his hearing, his sight, his limbs, his speech, his breath, his walk, etc. This state is the plenary good that God speaks of in chapter *The Cow*:

He gives the wisdom unto whom He pleases and whosoever the

wisdom is given to, he indeed is given a lot of good but none does remember except the people of the living heart. (The Quran, chapter *The Cow*, 2:269)

The Universal Scale

Wisdom also entails recognizing how various factors relate to one another, whether they be on a smaller, larger or even universal scale. Universal wisdom is known as the higher wisdom (*al ḥikma al 'uliyā*), or the supreme intellect (*al 'aql al akbar*). It refers to the realization of the supreme law by which the entire universe is governed. The fundamental principles of that law do not change in themselves —they are applicable at all times and all places. The dynamics of those principles, on the other hand, do change as a result of the cyclical expansions of the universe, causing a shift in the dimensions and the proportions of former existing relationships.

And the heaven, We built it with power and truly We certainly are expanding it. (The Quran, chapter *The Scatterers*, 51:47)

Man's quest for wisdom is self-fulfilling because it is only by learning wisdom that he will find harmony and peace in his own existence. It is wisdom that teaches us how to measure and balance through which we know our rights and duties on others and vice versa. If we receive our rights and fulfill our duties, we will live in a harmonious relationship with those around us. Wisdom, therefore, lies in giving everyone who has a right their right without excess or shortcoming. In other words, wisdom is the dispensation of truth justly and fairly to all concerned. Hence, in Semitic languages, such as Arabic and Hebrew, the word for wisdom is *ḥikmat*. This is a compound word from *hik/hiq*, which means "right," "measure," and "share;" and *mat*, which means "middle," "just," and "equitable." Thus, *ḥikmat* is the fair dispensation of rights. Furthermore, the word for truth and right is the same: *ḥaqq*.

The Principles of Wisdom

The *first* principle of wisdom is to recognize the right of God. Undoubtedly, the first and foremost of all the rights is that of the Creator. No person who denies His right can be deemed as truly wise. The Prophet Muhammad, peace be upon him, said, "The right of Allah over His servants is that they adore Him and make no partners with Him. Their right over

Him is that once they worship Him, and Him alone, He will bless them and safeguard them from fire" (Bukhari).

Thus, recognizing the right of God upon us, our duty towards Him, and our right over Him, constitutes the first principle of wisdom. Through the recognition of these mutual rights, we thus establish a harmonious relationship between the Divine and the human.

The *second* principle of wisdom is to regulate our relationship with our kinsfolk, beginning with our parents; which is why they are always mentioned after God, followed by spouses, children, siblings, etc.

The *third* principle of wisdom is regarding our relationship with our own selves: the right of our soul towards us and our duties towards it. As the Prophet Muhammad, peace be upon him, said, "Your soul has a right over you" (Bukhari)

The *fourth* principle is regarding our relationship with the larger society:

> Except those who believed and did righteous deeds and who exhorted one another to the truth and who exhorted one another to the patience. (The Quran, chapter *The Age*, 103:3)

> And above all, he was among those who believed and mutually enjoined the patience and mutually enjoined the mercy. (The Quran, chapter *The City*, 90:17)

The *fifth* principle of wisdom is based on our relationship to the universe as a whole. It teaches us the supreme wisdom: the key that unlocks the doors to the various mysteries, defined by God as "plenty of good" in the following verse:

> He gives wisdom unto whom He pleases and whosoever the wisdom is given to, he indeed is given a lot of good, but none does remember except the people of the heart. (The Quran, chapter *The Cow*, 2:269)

Plenty of good here means good that is infinite.

With this in mind, one of the most important assignments given to the Prophets, peace be upon them, is to teach wisdom after learning it themselves. This is in keeping with their mandate to teach people about the Truth, which is, by definition, what is good and lasting. In other words, their mission is to educate people about God, the origin of everything that is good and lasting:

> And do not stretch your gaze unto that which We have provided to some kinds of them as a temporary enjoyment, as a flowering of the life of this world, so that We may try them thereby, and provision of your Lord is better and more lasting. (The Quran, chapter *Taha*, 20:131)

> But the hereafter is better and more lasting. (The Quran, chapter *The Most High*, 87:17)

Having thus introduced the general principles of wisdom we may now proceed to analyze the wisdom granted by God to various individuals among His blessed servants in order to integrate their teachings into our own lives.

PART I

THE WISDOM OF LUQMAN

The 1ˢᵗ Principle: The Right of God

W e will begin with the wisdom of Luqman because, although brief, it contains all of the elements of genuine wisdom.

When God the Almighty bestowed wisdom on Luqman, He admonished him to show gratitude for this priceless gift by publicizing it and sharing it with others. Luqman decided that the first person he would share his wisdom with would be his son, as charity is supposed to begin at home. Thus, he laid out the fundamental principles of wisdom to his son, beginning with the first and the foremost: one's duty towards God.

> And when Luqman said to his son while he admonished him, "O my son! Do not ascribe partners to Allah. Truly ascribing partners to Allah is an egregious wrongdoing." (The Quran, chapter *Luqman*, 31:13)

He thus impressed upon his son the preeminence of God's right in comparison to all others, which is also the right from which all other rights derive. God's sole right is to be worshiped alone and that right is indivisible; it is all His. He is true in His essence and true in His attributes. In His essence, nothing is like Him and by His attributes, everything is. Hence, the meaning of the verse:

> Originator of the heavens and of the earth. He has made for you pairs from yourselves and pairs from the cattle. Through it, He multiplies you. There is nothing like Him and He is The All-Hearing,

The All-Seeing. (The Quran, chapter *The Consultation*, 42:11)

> There is nothing like Him in His essence and true existence belongs only to Him; nothing else exists in relation to His essence. The creation exist only in relation to His attributes, hence the ending of the verse - "He is The All-Hearing, The All-Seeing." (The Quran, chapter *The Consultation*, 42:11)

Similarly, in chapter *The Human Being*, God says:

> We indeed created the human being from a mixture of fluids that we may try him, so We made him hearing and seeing. (The Quran, chapter *The Human Being*, 76:2)

These attributes in general belong in two categories: magnificence and grandeur. Thus, the Prophet, peace be upon him, described God's attributes as dresses, saying, "Allah said: 'Grandeur is My cloak and magnificence is My mantle'" (*Fourty Ḥadīth Qudsiy*). His attributes are like His dresses through which His essence shines forth, taking the shape, the colour, and the proportions of the dress, either majestic or beautiful. His attributes, are the veil of His essence and through them, everything came to exist.

We must therefore be aware of the details regarding His essence and attributes in order to be able to relate to Him harmoniously and respond to Him accurately. In this realization lies the heart of true worship.

> And I have not created the Jinns and humankind except that they serve Me (in truth). (The Quran, chapter *The Scatterers*, 51:56)

CHAPTER 2

The 2nd Principle: The Right of Parents

L uqman then goes on to teach his son about the second principle of wisdom, which is concerned with the rights of the kinsfolk.

And We have exhorted the human being regarding his parents. His mother carried him in weakness upon weakness and his weaning is in two years. So offer gratitude to Me and to your parents and unto Me is the place of final coming. But if they urge you to ascribe such things as partners to Me for which you have no knowledge, then obey them not, but keep them a goodly company in this world and follow the way of one who has turned back to Me. Then unto Me will be your return and I will inform you about all that you used to do. (The Quran, chapter *Luqman*, 31:14-15)

In this principle, God begins with the rights of parents because it is through them that God brought us forth into this world. We cannot live our life in harmony if we neglect our connection with them. He also highlights the role of the mother because she went through untold hardships during pregnancy, and in giving birth. The water of life from which we enter this world, comes from our mothers, and therefore, we still carry a piece of our mothers within us. Thus, our duty towards them is to remember them and be grateful as best as we can. Here remembering specifically means praying for them whenever they cross our minds. In this respect, God taught us to say:

O my Lord, bestow your mercy on both of them as they raised me when I was small. (The Quran, chapter *The Night Journey*, 17:24)

Being grateful means to please them as best as we can. Praying for them and pleasing them is acting in excellence towards them (*ihsān*). Failing to do so is incurring wrongfulness (*zulm*), and God loves not the wrongdoers (*zālimīn*):

> If pain touches you, then indeed pain touched the people like unto it. And those days, we rotate between people and so that Allah may mark out those who believe and that He may take out the witnesses from among you, and Allah loves not those who wrong their own souls. (The Quran, chapter *The Family of Imran*, 3:140)

Conversely, God loves those who act with excellence by giving everyone and everything their right in full:

> Those who spend in the time of ease and in the time of hardship and keep in check the rage and pardon the people, and Allah loves those who act in excellence (The Quran, chapter *The Family of Imran*, 3:134)

Seeking to attain excellence in everything we do is the purpose of our existence.

> He who created death and life so that He may try you and mark out who among you is most excellent in work, and He it is The Almighty, The Oft-Forgiving. (The Quran, chapter *The Dominion*, 67:2)

It is reported that Zain al-'Abideen 'Ali, son of Hussain, the son of 'Ali and Fatimah, may God be pleased with them all, used to refrain from eating with his mother, and when he was asked about that, he said, "I fear to displease her by taking a piece of meat or morsel of food which she might have liked to take" (Ibn Al Athir, Ibn Kathir). It is also reported in the life story (*sīra*) of the Prophet Muhammad, peace be upon him, that on one of his travels from Mecca to Medina, he stopped on the way to pay a visit to the tomb of his mother, Aminah, may God's mercy be with her, and when he came back to his companions, his eyes were filled with tears. So they asked him, "O Messenger of Allah, what makes you cry so that if we know the reason, we may also weep?" He replied, "I asked my Lord to permit me to visit the grave of my mother. He permitted me, and I asked Him to permit me to ask forgiveness for her (*maghfira*) and He did not. I thus was overcome with filial emotions" (Muslim).

The reason for withholding permission is that the Prophet, peace be upon him, was the role model for his companions and generations after them, and they were categorically forbidden to advocate on behalf of those who were deceased and had ascribed partners to God:

> It is not right for the Prophet and for those who believe to ask for forgiveness for those who ascribe partners unto Allah, even if they may be their near of kin, after it has become evident for them that they indeed are people of the hellfire. Abraham's asking for forgiveness for his father was but a result of a promise that he promised him, but when it became evident to him that he indeed was an enemy to Allah, then he disavowed him. Truly, Abraham surely was oft-imploring magnanimous. (The Quran, chapter *The Repentance*, 9:113-14)

Both John and Jesus son of Mary, were given direct instructions from God to observe kindness to their parents as part of the wisdom given unto them:

> "O Yahya! Hold the book with all your strength and We had given him the wisdom while still a child. And [he was granted] tenderness from Our presence and purity, and he was reverent to Allah. And kind to his parents and never was he overbearing, disobedient. (The Quran, chapter *Mary*, 19:12-14)

> He said, "I am a slave of Allah and He has given me the book and He has made me a prophet, And He has made me blessed wheresoever I may be, and He has admonished me to prayer and to self-purification as long as I am alive. And He has made me kind to my mother and has not made me overbearing, miserable." (The Quran, chapter *Mary*, 19:30-32)

God's Right

The rights of parents must stop where God's right begins and if they, in any way, urge you to violate the right of God by going against His commandment, then you are not to obey them. That refusal to obey, however, must be conducted with extreme tenderness, care, love and respect:

But if they [your parents] urge you to ascribe such things as partners to Me for which you have no knowledge, then obey them not,
but keep them a goodly company in this world and follow the way
of one who has turned back to Me. Then unto Me will be your return and I will inform you about all that you used to do. (The Quran, chapter *Luqman*, 31:15)

And We have enjoined unto the mankind that he should be kind to
his parents, but if they force you to ascribe as a partner to Me such
a thing about which you have no knowledge, then obey them not.
Your place of return is unto Me and then I will inform you about all
that you used to do. (The Quran, chapter *The Spider*, 29:8)

We have commanded unto the human being kindness to his parents. His mother born him with hardship and laid him down with
hardship and his bearing and his weaning is thirty months, until
when he reaches the fullness of his strength and reaches forty years,
he says, "O my Lord! Exhort me so that I give gratitude for your
blessing with which you blessed me and both of my parents, and
that I work righteous deeds which may please You and put righteousness for me in my descendants. Truly, I have turned to You
in repentance and truly I am of those who have submitted to you."
Those are the ones from whom We accept the best of what they
worked and We forego their evil deeds [to be] among the owners of
the garden, the truthful promise of which they used to be promised.
As for the one who says to his parents, "Fie unto both of you. Do
both of you promise me that I will be brought forth [after death]
when the generations had passed before me?" But the two of them
seek the help of Allah [and they say], "Woe unto you! Believe! Truly, Allah's promise is true." But he says, "This is nothing but the fa-
bles of the ancients." (The Quran, chapter *The Winding Sand Tracts*,
46:15-18)

It should be borne in mind that being required to express tenderness, care,
love and respect to someone does not stipulate following them. If your parents do not know, you are required to love them, but not to follow them.
You must only follow the one who knows and has the criterion (*furqān*). In
this respect, God says:

And do not follow that which you have no knowledge [certitude] for. Truly, the hearing and the sight and the understanding, all of that are going to be questioned about. (The Quran, chapter *The Night Journey*, 17:36)

Furthermore, Prophet Abraham (Ibrahim), peace be upon him, says to his father:

"O my father, something from the knowledge has indeed come to me that has not come to you; therefore, follow me and I will guide you to a way that is midmost." (The Quran, chapter *Mary*, 19:43)

This notion is similarly expressed in Luqman's advice to his son:

But if they [your parents] urge you to ascribe such things as partners to Me for which you have no knowledge, then obey them not, but keep them a goodly company in this world and follow the way of one who has turned back to Me. Then unto Me will be your return and I will inform you about all that you used to do. (The Quran, chapter *Luqman*, 31:15)

If it so happens that one or both of your parents is a person of knowledge, then you owe them love as a filial obligation, as well as obedience and submission for one who has criterion, and you must follow them.

O you who believe! Obey Allah and obey the messenger and the people of the commandment among you. But if you disagree about anything, then refer it back to Allah and to the messenger if you indeed believe in Allah and in the last day. That is better and most excellent in interpretation. (The Quran, chapter *The Women*, 4:59)

To Moses (Musa) and Aaron (Haroon), peace be upon them, God says:

"Your invocation has indeed been answered; therefore, stand upright, both of you, and follow not both of you the way of those who do not know." (The Quran, chapter *Jonah*, 10:89)

Furthermore, God refutes the argument of those who say, "We only follow in the footsteps of our fathers," even though their fathers had no knowledge.

> Follow that which has been revealed unto you from your Lord. There is no deity save He and turn away from those who ascribe partners to Him. (The Quran, chapter *The Cattle*, 6:106)

> And when it is said unto them, "Follow that which Allah has sent down." They say, "Nay, we will continue to follow what we found our fathers on." What? Even if their fathers understood nothing, nor were they well-guided? (The Quran, chapter *The Cow*, 2:170)

> And when it is said unto them, "Follow that which Allah has sent down," they say, "Nay! We follow that which we have found our fathers on." What! Even though it is Satan calling them to the punishment of a blazing fire? (The Quran, chapter *Luqman*, 31:21)

It is clear that you should not follow your parents if they do not know, yet the fact that they do not know is no justification to deprive them of their right to kind treatment, respect, and love.

CHAPTER 3

The 3ʳᵈ Principle: The Right of One's Soul

The third principle is concerned with the relationship between a person and his or her own soul. It describes the
duty of a person towards their own souls and the rights of
their souls over them. It should be neither overworked nor underworked:
no person has the right to wrong his or her own soul by putting a burden on
it that it cannot bear, because this hinders its growth from excellence, nor
can one deprive it of its opportunity for growth by underworking it.

Allah does not charge a soul with more than its capacity. For it is all
that it has earned and against it is all that it has perpetrated. O our
Lord! Do not take us to task if we forget or we make mistakes. O our
Lord! And do not put upon us a burden like one You put upon those
before us. O our Lord! And do not burden us with what we have no
strength to bear and pardon us and forgive us and have mercy on
us. You are our Master, so help us against the disbelieving people.
(The Quran, chapter *The Cow*, 2:286)

The Balanced Diet

The soul should be kept on a balanced diet that is neither austere
nor extravagant. Additionally, it should be sustained with a balanced rou-
tine between sleep and waking; sleep for rest and recuperation, and waking
for work to seek the bounties of God.

And among His signs is your sleep [rest] by night and by day and
your seeking [by night and by day] from His favor. Truly in that are
signs for people who hear. (The Quran, chapter *The Romans*, 30:23)

And out of His mercy, He has made the night and the day for you
so that you may find rest in it and that you may seek from His favor and perhaps that you may be grateful. (The Quran, chapter *The
Stories*, 28:73)

The Soul's Travel

The essence of the fourth principle is to pace the soul moderately
between station and travel. The soul is thus presented as a means of trans-
port for a person; it requires rest after travel and travel after rest until it
reaches its destination safe and sound. If you overwork your soul, or if you
tarry too long at resting stations, it will die before it reaches its destination.

And He it is who raised you from one life with a place of ultimate
station and a place of original station. We indeed have detailed the
signs for a people who have discernment. (The Quran, chapter *The
Cattle*, 6:98)

There is no creature that moves in the earth but surely its suste-
nance is binding upon Allah and He knows its place and time of rest
and its place and time of motion, all in a clear book. (The Quran,
chapter *Hud*, 11:6)

In this regard, there is a prophetic narration which says, "This religion is solid; therefore, make yourself into it with gentleness, for the person
who rides their horse too fast neither makes it to the end nor keeps their
ride alive" (Tirmidhi). The Prophet Muhammad, peace be upon him, thus
describes the person who has overworked his or her soul as killing it, and
in the end, never reaches their destination.

The Soul's Provision and Reckoning

The provision that is destined for someone will surely come to
them no matter where it happens to be found: in the heavens, in the earth,
or in a rock. If you are in the heavens, your provision is in the heavens with
you. If you are in the earth, your provision is with you in the earth. If you
are in a mountain, your provision will be with you in that mountain. God
has measured your provision with the vicissitudes of your soul and it will
catch up with you wherever you happen to be; your haste or your tarrying

will not affect its timing. Wherever you are, God's knowledge (*Al-Khabīr*) is with you, as well as His imperceptible Gentleness (*Al-Laṭīf*), as stated in chapter *Luqman*:

> "O my son, were it but the weight of the seed of mustard and it were in a rock or in the heavens or in the earth, Allah will bring it. Truly, Allah is All-Subtle, All-Acquainted." (The Quran, chapter *Luqman*, 31:16)

This verse has two interpretations. First, that wherever your provision lies, whether it be in a rock or in the heavens or in the earth, it will find you since God is All-Acquainted with your conditions and Gentle in channeling the provisions to you. In other words, wherever your provisions are, your provisions will catch up with you, for as much as His Knowledge is with you, so is His Mercy.

> Wherever you may be, death will overtake you, even if you were in towers raised aloft. And when a good thing happens to them, they said, "This is from the presence of Allah," and when an evil thing happens to them, they said, "This is from your side." Say, "All is from the presence of Allah." Why is it that these people almost do not comprehend any discourse? (The Quran, chapter *The Women*, 4:78)

Second, it implies that God has measured everything and nothing is allowed to go missing, whether it be in a rock or in the heavens or in the earth; God will bring it and lay it on the scale on the Day of Judgment, for every soul must account for every single blessing of God, from wherever it originated. It will be only through His subtle Gentleness that a believer will find reprieve from the rigors of that reckoning.

Thus, whatever a soul does, whether it is an atom size of good or of evil, it will have to account for it.

> So that whoever does an atom's weight of a good deed will see it. And whoever does an atom's weight of an evil deed will see it. (The Quran, chapter *The Utmost Shaking*, 99:7-8)

To keep a middle course, we must not offer unto our souls more than what is due to them, nor give them less than what is due to them. In all of this, we must keep in mind that it is only through God's gentle grace that we can fulfill that balance, not through personal judiciousness. Therefore, we must endeavor with the utmost endeavoring to keep this strict balance with regards to our souls, for someone who is expecting that they will be reckoned for everything they do will surely try to be as excellent as they can be in their deeds. And whoever does expecting their reckoning will care about what they do.

> And those who keep fast that which Allah has commanded to be joined and hold their Lord in deference and fear a woeful reckoning. (The Quran, chapter *The Thunder*, 13:21)

> Say, "I am but a human being, the best model for you, and I am divinely inspired. Truly, your deity is only one deity and whoever looks forward to meeting his Lord, let him therefore do righteous deed and ascribe none else as partner in the worship of his Lord." (The Quran, chapter *The Cave*, 18:110)

> And whoever expects meeting with Allah, then truly the appointed term of Allah is surely going to come and He is The All-Hearing, The All-Knowing. (The Quran, chapter *The Spider*, 29:5)

And seek help through patience and prayer, and truly, it is surely hard except on those who are humble.

> Who expect that they are going to meet their Lord and that they indeed are going to return to Him. (The Quran, chapter *The Cow*, 2:45-46)

Surely, one who is expecting to meet their Lord will try their level best to act excellently, and if there are any shortcomings, their Lord will fulfill their measure and grant them from His favour. This is because such people maintained a balance between fear of His reckoning and hope in His favour.

> And their flanks shun their beds. They call out to their Lord out of fear and hope, and they spend out of that which We have provided them with. (The Quran, chapter *The Prostration*, 32:16)

> And those who give what they give while their hearts are in tremor

[knowing] that they are going to return to their Lord. (The Quran, chapter *The Believers*, 23:60)

So whoever is given his book in his right hand then he will be reckoned with an easy reckoning, and he will return to his people rejoicing, but whosoever is given his book behind his back, he then is going to call out for annihilation, And he will burn in a blazing fire. (The Quran, chapter *The Breaking Up*, 84:7-12)

There is reckoning in all cases, whether the book is in the left or the right, except that there is gentleness in one and none in the other. That gentleness derives from their combined faith in God's Mercy whilst expecting requital for their deeds. A prophetic tradition makes this point clear: "Whoever fasts Ramadan with faith and with expectations for requital, they will be forgiven all their past sins" (Bukhari).

CHAPTER 4

The 4th Principle: The Right of Society

The fourth principle of wisdom pertains to social reform, which defines one's relationship with society, and specifically his or her duty towards it and its right over him or her. Such endeavors keep in view God's plan to send human beings as vice-regents on earth in order to establish a human community that is guided through the commandments of God. With this end in mind, the objective is to fulfill the purpose for which God has empowered human beings on the earth with.

> And indeed We have established you in the earth and We have made for you therein livelihood. How little is that you offer gratitude. (The Quran, chapter *The Heights*, 7:10)

Such an empowerment was not meant for its own sake, but rather to free human beings for the ultimate purpose of their existence, which is to know the truth and to find happiness.

> It is those who when We establish them in the earth, they establish the prayer and they give out the sanctifying dues and they enjoin [others] to do righteous things and forbid [them] from doing wicked things, and for Allah is the ending of all matters. (The Quran, chapter *The Pilgrimage*, 22:41)

These are the reasons God placed Adam's children on the earth: to establish God's remembrance; to share the blessings of God, which He has spread all over the earth; to fight the causes of greed and avarice; to admonish one another to give others their right and acquit themselves of their duties; and to refrain from cheating others of their rights.

> By the age. Truly the human being is surely in loss. Except those
> who believed and did righteous deeds and who exhorted one an-
> other to the truth and who exhorted one another to patience. (The
> Quran, chapter *The Age*, 103:1-3)

> And above all, he was among those who believed and mutually en-
> joined patience and mutually enjoined mercy. (The Quran, chapter
> *The City*, 90:17)

The Tools of Social Reform: Patience and Prayer

The word truth (*ḥaqq*) also means right; thus, the previous verses
mean enjoining one another to give everyone's right to them, beginning
with the right of God, followed by the right of the parents, the right of the
self, the right of the orphan, the right of the needy and the poor, etc. Besides
enjoining one another to give rights and take rights, we are also enjoined to
be patient and merciful. Patience is useful when we are wronged or cheated.
We should not respond with anger nor be hasty in action; rather, we should
remain peaceful and steadfast until our right is restored.

> And the price for ill is ill like unto it, but one who pardons and
> amends, indeed his reward is upon Allah. Truly, He does not love
> the wrongdoers. And surely whoever makes resistance for himself
> after wrong has been done to him, for those indeed there is no way
> against them. The way is only against those who wrong the people
> and who seek to trespass in the earth without the truth. Truly, those
> for them there will be a painful punishment. And truly one who ex-
> ercises patience and forgives, that indeed is surely among the most
> resolute affairs. (The Quran, chapter *The Consultation*, 42:40-43)

> And if you meet out a punishment, then afflict a punishment of
> the like of that which you are punished with, but if you exercise
> patience, truly that [patience] is best for those who are patient. (The
> Quran, chapter *The Bee*, 16:126)

A task of social reform cannot be accomplished single handedly. It
requires the concurrence and the concerted efforts of numerous individuals
who are patient and steadfast in their prayers. Prayer, in essence, means

remembrance of God.

> Truly, I am Allah. There is no deity except I. Therefore, serve Me and establish the prayer for My remembrance. (The Quran, chapter *Taha*, 20:14)

When God sent Moses and Aaron, peace be upon them, to the Pharaoh, God said unto Moses:

> Go forth you and your brother with My signs and do not tire both of you in remembering Me. (The Quran, chapter *Taha*, 20:42)

In essence, the meaning of the verse is to be steadfast in His remembrance. Surely, one who is not steadfast in the remembrance of God cannot overcome the trials and tribulations that lay across his path. Therefore, it is only through the concerted efforts of multiple individuals who are patient and steadfast in their prayers that any significant social reform can take place.

> And seek help through patience and prayer; truly, it is surely hard except on those who are humble. (The Quran, chapter *The Cow*, 2:45)

> O you who believe! Do not violate the rights of Allah nor the sacred month nor the consecrated gifts nor the garlanded animals nor those who are aiming for the sacred house seeking the bounty from their Lord and goodly pleasure. But once you are free from the pilgrimage rituals, then hunt, and let not the hatred of people incite you to evildoing only because they had barred you from the sacred mosque, that you transgress [against them]. And assist one another unto piety and unto Allah's reverence, and do not assist one another unto impiety and unto transgression, and revere Allah. Truly, Allah is severe in chastisement. (The Quran, chapter *The Heavenly Food Bowl*, 5:2)

> O you who believe! When you hold secret counsels among you, do not counsel one another unto sinfulness and transgression and disobedience of the messenger; rather, counsel one another unto piety and self-guard. And revere Allah unto whom you shall be gathered. (The Quran, chapter *The Arguing Woman*, 58:9)

O you who believe! Be patient and exhort one another unto patience and re-comfort one another and revere Allah so that perhaps you may prosper. (The Quran, chapter *The Family of Imran*, 3:200)

In other verses, we get further clarification of the meaning of patience, referred to as *thubūt*, which means holding your ground and not turning back on your heels.

O you who believe! When you meet a band in war, do hold your ground and remember Allah a great deal so that perhaps you may prosper. (The Quran, chapter *The Gains of War*, 8:45)

Calling Unto the Way of God

Luqman communicated this fourth principle of wisdom to his son by saying to him:

"O my son! Establish the prayer and command unto kindness and forbid from meanness and bear with patience whatever happens to you. Truly that is among the most resolute of all the affairs." (The Quran, chapter *Luqman*, 31:17)

Here, Luqman is advising his son that if he wishes to take on the task of calling people to the way of God (*da'wa*), then the first and foremost requirement is to establish his prayer — meaning be steadfast in the remembrance of God. He advised him to lead by example, so that before he calls people unto something, he must be the first person to act on it.

Thus, the first commandment revealed from the Quran is to read:

Read by the name of your Lord, He who created. He created the human being from congealed blood. Read! And your Lord, The All-Gracious; He who taught through the pen. He taught the human being that which he knew not. (The Quran, chapter *The Congealed Blood*, 96:1-5)

The next commandment is to establish prayer:

O you the one wrapped. Stand for prayer through the night except for a little Half of or it or make it a little less than that. Or make it more than that and recite the Quran with a careful recitation. We indeed are soon going to deliver unto you a weighty word. Truly the growing hours of the night are greater in impact and most upright in speech. Truly in the day there is for you a lengthy course of adoration. And remember the name of your Lord and devote yourself to Him with a whole devotion; Lord of the East and of the West. There is no deity except He; therefore, take Him as a trustee. And bear with patience all that they say and forsake them with a nicely forsaking. (The Quran, chapter *The One Wrapped*, 73:1-10)

The next commandment is to go out and call people to the way of truth:

O you the one wrapped in cloak, Rise up and warn. And your Lord! Do proclaim His greatness. And your garment, keep it clean. And the abominations, do forsake. And do not boast about your gifts in order to seek aggrandizement for yourself. And for your Lord, be patient. (The Quran, chapter *The One Wrapped in Cloak*, 74:1-7)

There are three phases a caller (*dā'ī*) must go through to succeed: 1. In-depth study of the book (Quran); 2. Establishing prayers, both obligatory and voluntary; and 3. To walk among their fellow human beings spreading glad tidings and warning.

Those who call people to the word of God are truly the viceregents of God on the earth. God promises them — and His promise is true — that He will establish them on the earth and establish their religion.

Allah has promised those who believe and do righteous deeds from among you that He will surely appoint them as viceregents in the earth, as He did appoint those before them as viceregents, and He will surely establish for them their religion, which He has chosen for them out of His Pleasure, and He will most certainly give them security in replacement for their fear. They must then worship Me and ascribe nothing as partner to Me and whosoever turns to disbelief after that, truly it is they who are the renegades. (The Quran, chapter *The Light*, 24:55)

The *dā'ī*, in his zeal to call people to the way of God, must always bear in mind that he can only call people with the permission (*idhn*) of God and therefore, compulsion is not necessary. All he has to do is deliver the

message concisely and clearly, and then God will guide whom He pleases
and let go astray whom He pleases.

> Had your Lord so willed, then surely everyone in the earth - all of
> them together - would have believed. Are you then going to compel
> people until they become believers? It is not [possible] for a soul to
> believe except by the leave of Allah, and He heaps up infamy upon
> those who do not understand. (The Quran, chapter *Jonah*, 10:99-
> 100)

> Truly, You guide not whom You love, but Allah guides whom He
> pleases, and it is He who knows best about those who are on the
> right guidance. (The Quran, chapter *The Stories*, 28:56)

These reminders take a huge burden off the shoulders of the caller, since
they do not have to exert themselves beyond their limit.

> Is the one whose evil deed is made to look goodly in his eyes so that
> he sees it as an excellent deed [equal to the one who is well guided
> by Allah]? Truly, Allah allows to go astray whom He pleases and
> guides whom He pleases, so do not let your soul grieve over them.
> Truly, Allah is All-Knowing about all that they fabricate. (The Qu-
> ran, chapter *Originator of Creation*, 35:8)

> And perhaps you are going to torment your soul with grief chas-
> ing after them if they do not believe in this discourse. (The Quran,
> chapter *The Cave*, 18:6)

> Perhaps you are going to vex yourself that they are not believers [in
> this book]. (The Quran, chapter *The Poets*, 26:3)

For such and many other reasons, the caller must remain steadfast and not
be swayed by the negative responses he receives from people, since he is
only meant to call them, and is not in charge of them.

> So turn away from them and you are not to be blamed. But remind;
> truly the reminding does benefit the believers. (The Quran, chapter
> *The Scatterers*, 51:54-55)

Therefore remind, for you are but one who reminds.

You are not put in charge over them. (The Quran, chapter *The Over-whelming Event*, 88:21-22)

We do know about all that they say, but you are not a compeller over them, so remind them through the Quran whosoever fears My warning. (The Quran, chapter *Qaf*, 50:45)

And had Allah so willed, they would not have ascribed partners to Him, and We have not appointed you as a guardian over them, nor are you in charge of them. (The Quran, chapter *The Cattle*, 6:107)

Calling the People of the Book

God has set out a separate body of ethics with regards to calling the people of the book to the way of God. Like any other kind of call, it must be conducted with wisdom and kind admonishing, and one must argue with them only in a way that is most excellent. God explains what most excellent means:

Call unto the way of your Lord with wisdom and with a goodly preaching and argue with them only with that which is the most excellent. Truly your Lord is He who knows best who has gone astray from His way and it is He who knows best who are well guided. (The Quran, chapter *The Bee*, 16:125)

And do not dispute with the people of the book except through that which is most excellent apart from those who among them have wronged their own souls, and say, "We believe in that which has been sent down to us and which has been sent down to you, and our God and your God is one, but we have submitted to Him." (The Quran, chapter *The Spider*, 29:46)

Say, "O people of the scripture! Come unto a word that is common between us and you, that we should worship none except Allah and that we should ascribe nothing as a partner with Him and that some of us do not take others as Lords besides Allah." But if they turn away, then say, "Bear witness that we indeed are those who have submitted to Allah." (The Quran, chapter *The Family of Imran*, 3:64)

In light of the foregoing verses, calling the people of the book should be centered around the significance of the word *islām* or *taslīm*. It must be stressed that a Muslim is no different than a Christian or a Jew except in one thing: that he has chosen to surrender his entire being unto God. The least we can say is that one who chooses to be a Muslim aims at this end — even though he may or may not succeed in realizing it. It is sufficient for a person to strive and intend to attain this state, with the understanding that God ultimately determines outcomes. As the Prophet, peace be upon him, stated, "Allah does not look at your figures, nor at your attire, but He looks at your hearts [and deeds]," meaning your intention and action (Muslim).

Unity over difference in the matter of religion must be highlighted to bring the ranks closer between Muslims and people of the book. Prophet Muhammad, peace be upon him, endeavored to realize this objective by sending some of his companions to a Christian king in Abyssinia and by drawing a peace treaty with the Jews when he migrated to Medina. In all of this, the Prophet, peace be upon him, stressed what is common rather than what is different. Sharing our unity first — belief in one God and the revealed books — is at the core of wisdom when inviting the people of the book to a common ground. After that, the Muslim has the freedom to pursue what is unique to them, namely self-surrender to God.

The term *muslim* is itself explained by God with another term *mukhliṣ*, which comes from the root word *ikhlāṣ*, meaning something that is undivided and unmixed. Therefore, a Muslim is a *mukhliṣ* whose faith in God is undivided and unmixed. He undividedly serves only God and no other master; he undividedly believes in everything that comes from God, and he does not mix God's Word, which is the truth, with anyone else's word. He also brings all his matters back to God; and when God makes a judgment, he accepts it wholeheartedly. These are some of the definitions of the word *ikhlāṣ* in the Quran:

> Truly, We have revealed this book unto you by the truth so worship Allah while making the religion sincere only for Him. Truly, the sincere religion is for Allah only, but those who have taken allies besides Him [they say], "We worship them not except that they may bring us very close to Allah." Truly, Allah will judge between them with wisdom in all that wherein they differ. Truly, Allah does not guide one who is a liar, ungrateful. Had Allah willed to take [unto

Himself] a son, truly He would have chosen that which He pleases from whatever he creates. Glory be unto Him. He is Allah, The One, The All-Over-powering. (The Quran, chapter *The Flocks*, 39:2-4)

Say, "I indeed am commanded to worship Allah, making the religion sincere for Him." And I have been commanded that I should be of the first of those who have submitted themselves to Allah. (The Quran, chapter *The Flocks*, 39:11-12)

Is he whose bosom Allah has expanded towards self-submission [for Allah] so that he is on a light from his Lord [not better guided]? But woe unto those whose hearts are hard towards the remembrance of Allah. Those are in misguidance most evident. (The Quran, chapter *The Flocks*, 39:22)

Allah has set forth a parable: a man who is owned by partners who are at variance with one another and a man who is wholly dedicated to one man. Are the two equal in similitude? The praise is for Allah. Nay, most of them do not know. (The Quran, chapter *The Flocks*, 39:29)

And when Allah all alone is mentioned, the hearts of those who do not believe in the hereafter feel repugnant, but when those besides Him [whom they have taken as partners] are mentioned, lo! They are filled with joy. (The Quran, chapter *The Flocks*, 39:45)

And they said, "Be people of Judaism," or, "Be Christian;" then, you will be rightly-guided. Say, "Nay, rather follow the way of Abraham, who turned away from all else and he was not of those who ascribe partners to Allah." (The Quran, chapter *The Cow*, 2:135)

Say, "Are you disputing with us about Allah while He is our Lord and your Lord, and for us are our deeds and for your are your deeds, while we make our religion sincere for Him." (The Quran, chapter *The Cow*, 2:139)

The Middle Nation

Furthermore, God describes those who adhere to the religion of self-surrender as a nation of the middle, *ummatan wasaṭan*, who do not belong to any religious factions, but who keep a middle course. From this vantage point, they serve as witnesses over all other nations.

And thus We have appointed you a nation of just middle so that you may be witnesses over mankind and that the messenger may be a witness over you. And We did not appoint the direction on which you were before except for the purpose that We may mark out who follows the messenger from him who turns back on his heels. And truly, it surely was a hard test except for those whom Allah guided. And Allah surely was not going to let your faith go in waste. Truly, Allah is surely All-Tender, Most-Merciful for mankind. (The Quran, chapter *The Cow*, 2:143)

Similarly, God urges the Messenger, peace be upon him, to maintain an unbiased opinion between the people of the book:

Therefore, do call unto that and stand upright as you have been commanded and do not follow their vain desires and say, "I believe in all books that Allah has sent down and I have been commanded to be just between you. Allah is our Lord and your Lord. For us are our deeds and for you your deeds. There is no recrimination between us and you. Allah will gather us altogether and unto Him is the place of final coming." (The Quran, chapter *The Consultation*, 42:15)

It must, however, be mentioned that belonging to this nation of the middle is not a birthright nor a religious protocol; rather, it is acquired by merit.

You indeed are best nation brought forth for mankind; you continue to command unto the kindness and you continue to forbid from the wickedness and you continue to believe in Allah. And had the people of scripture believed, it would surely have been better for them. Among them are the believers, but most of them are the renegades. (The Quran, chapter *The Family of Imran*, 3:110)

The term "best" is a conditional statement and not an absolute one; that is, you are the best nation when you strive the hardest in the way of God by admonishing people to give every owner of a right what is their right, as well as to be patient and steadfast, and to work as witnesses on the earth among your fellow human beings. Luqman was a member of the middle nation and wished his son to become one.

> "O my son! Establish the prayer and command unto kindness and forbid from meanness and bear with patience whatever happens to you. Truly, that is among the most resolute of all the affairs." (The Quran, chapter *Luqman*, 31:17)

Thus, belonging to the nation of the middle requires assiduity in prayer and forbearance in the face of provocation and hurt. The middle nation exists in some form or another on the earth at all times; the Prophet, peace be upon him, describes them in these terms: "There will always be a group from my nation who would have truth in sight until the end of time (until the coming of the Messiah)" (Muslim). That group is the middle nation who will always remain witnesses for God when the truth becomes hidden.

> And let there be among you a group who calls unto the good and they command unto the kindness and they forbid from the wickedness and those are the ones who have prospered. (The Quran, chapter *The Family of Imran*, 3:104)

The word *khayr* (good) in the verse refers to belief in God and the life of the hereafter.

> We truly believe in our Lord [hoping] that He will forgive us our faults and all that magic that you have compelled us to, and Allah is Best and is Most Lasting. (The Quran, chapter *Taha*, 20:73)

> But the hereafter is better and more lasting. (The Quran, chapter *The Most High*, 87:17)

CHAPTER 5

The 5ᵗʰ Principle: The Right of Society Via Balance

The wisdom of the balance is under the right of society. It is primarily concerned with keeping a delicate balance between gentleness and thoroughness. These two derive from God's characteristics, The All Subtle (*Al-Laṭīf*) and The All Acquainted (*Al-Khabīr*). This entirely translates into attempting to be as thorough as possible in self-reckoning as well as in administering justice to others, all the while without loosing sight of the fact that underneath that thoroughness and sternness in applying the divine decress lies the subtle gentleness.

The hard and coarse external shell must be cracked in order to reach the mercy beneath it. Thus, being stern and strict in administering the divine decree is itself a mercy because it leads to mercy. It is in this light that we must see the story of Moses and the guide when the guide cracked the ship, slew the boy, and raised the wall and said: "This is a mercy from my Lord." (Quran, chapter *The Cave*, 18:98). God's name, the All Acquainted (*Al-Khabīr*) requires thorough reckoning while His name *Al-Laṭīf*, reminds of the underlying gentleness and mercy.

CHAPTER 6

The 6th Principle: The Right of Society Via Peace

P eace, whether in word or in gesture, is an expression of humility and self-unrighteousness. This idea is conveyed in the wisdom of Luqman by the words:

> And do not turn your cheek arrogantly to men and do not walk in the earth exultantly. Truly Allah does not love the self-conceited and self-vaunting. (The Quran, chapter *Luqman*, 31:18)

This verse is further corroborated by the following verse in chapter *The Criterion*:

> And the servants of *Al-Raḥmān* are those who walk on the earth gently and when the ignorant ones address them, they say, "Peace." (The Quran, chapter *The Criterion*, 25:63)

These verses are both the expression of peace in words and in gesture. In sum, it is the right of society that one act in peace, and one does not respond to ignorance *with* ignorance. *"Peace"* should therefore be the response of a God-deferent person to both one who acts in ignorance or in peace.

CHAPTER 7

The 7th Principle: The Right of the Universe

The seventh principle of wisdom deals with our relationship with the universe. The fourth principle — *khilāfa* and our establishment in the earth — is only in preparation for our departure into the larger universe. The earth is just the launching ground.

> O you community of the Jinns and of the humans! If you are able to pass through the regions of the heavens and of the earth, then pass through. You will not pass except with an authority. (The Quran, chapter *The All-Merciful*, 55:33)

The "authority" in this verse refers to a spirit from God. It is a companion of the word, and when the Word is fulfilled, the authority is given from God. With the assistance of the authority, the bearer of the word will be able to overcome the various obstacles that will confront him, such as fire, air, water, and iron.

> Against both of you [without an authority] will be sent flames of fire and shower of iron so you will not triumph. (The Quran, chapter *The All-Merciful*, 55:35)

The Forces of Nature

In the Quran, God names some of His servants, like Abraham, Moses, Solomon (Sulayman), and David (Dawud) — may peace be upon them all — unto whom natural forces were subservient by virtue of the authority they were given from God. For Abraham, fire was made cool and peace:

They said, "Burn him and give victory to your gods if you are going to do something." We said, "O fire! Be cool and be peace upon Abraham." (The Quran, chapter *The Prophets*, 21:68-69)

For Moses, God says:

Thereupon, We inspired Moses, saying, "Strike the sea with your stick," so it [the sea] parted asunder and each part was like a magnificent mountain. (The Quran, chapter *The Poets*, 26:63)

With regards to David, God says:

And We have indeed given a favor unto David from Us, "O Mountains! Resonate with him and O you the birds [as well]! And We have softened the iron for him." (The Quran, chapter *The Kingdom of Saba*, 34:10)

Finally, with regards to Solomon, God says:

And for Solomon [We subjected] the wind [for him]; its morning [travel] is equal to a month's and its evening [travel] is equal to a month's and We caused a fount of molten brass to flow for him, and among the Jinns are those who work before him by the leave of his Lord, and whosoever among them swerves from Our commandment, We make them taste from the punishment of the blazing fire. (The Quran, chapter *The Kingdom of Saba*, 34:12)

The Role of Humility

God facilitates His servants' peregrinations in the various dimensions of the universe as they seek His bounties, which are disseminated across the world, while also rendering services wherever needed. Those who need help, they help them; those who need protection, they protect them. Where justice is needed, they administer justice; and where defense is needed, they establish the defense, such as in the story of Dhul Qarnain in chapter *The Cave* (18:83-98). In sum, their mandate is to spread peace and security as they journey across the universe.

And the servants of *Al-Raḥmān* are those who walk on the earth

gently and when the ignorant ones address them, they say, "Peace."
(The Quran, chapter *The Criterion*, 25:63)

This verse makes mention of the manner in which they walk. Their humble
manner of walking indicates the state of their heart. Only a knowing heart
is humble and appreciates God's supremeness above it. Thus, the humility
in their hearts that stems from this *knowing* flows out into the rest of their
being in the same manner that the physical heart pumps blood into the rest
of the body. They walk with gentleness, speak with gentleness, apprehend
with gentleness, and look with gentleness.

> Truly those who lower their voices in the presence of the messenger
> of Allah - those are the ones whose hearts Allah has well-tried for
> self-guard. For them is forgiveness and a magnificent reward. (The
> Quran, chapter *The Inner Apartments*, 49:3)

> And so both of you speak unto him a gentle word; perhaps, he may
> remember or defer [to His Lord]. (The Quran, chapter *Taha*, 20:44)

> That day, they will follow their caller in whom there is no crooked-
> ness, and all the voices are hushed for *Al-Raḥmān* [The All-Merci-
> ful], and you will hear nothing but whispers. (The Quran, chapter
> *Taha*, 20:108)

This all-pervading gentleness signifies that God-consciousness
has permeated through their whole being; each part of their being is aware
of its Lord and each particle in their being is knowing. In other words, their
whole being has become one knowing heart. In a *Ḥadīth Qudsiy* (divinely
inspired narraition) God says of such an individual, "I become his hearing
by which he hears, his sight by which he sees, his arm by which he appre-
hends, his feet by which he walks."

Luqman was admonishing his son to become such a servant of *Al-
Raḥmān*. He says to him:

> "And do not turn your cheek arrogantly to men and do not walk in
> the earth exultantly. Truly, Allah does not love any self-conceit and
> self-vaunting. And take a mid-course in your walk and lower from
> your voice. Truly, the most detestable of all sounds is the braying of
> the donkeys." (The Quran, chapter *Luqman*, 31:18-19)

He admonishes his son to show humility in all of his demeanors: to look at people with his full face and not sideways because that is a sign of arrogance. To not turn his back on them, because that is a sign of disregard. To not raise his voice, which annoys others. To not walk slowly or too quickly, but rather to be in synchrony with the cosmic pace. The cosmic pace means that your heart also beats in correspondence to the pace of the cosmic heartbeat. This is attained by means of the greatest remembrance: *dhikr al akbar*.

PART II

THE ROLE OF WISDOM WHEN TRAVELLING THE PATH

*Derived from the Prophet's Night Journey
(peace be upon him)*

CHAPTER 8

Wisdom and Gratitude

In the chapter *The Night Journey*, God says: That is from what your Lord has revealed unto you from wisdom; therefore, do not associate any other deity with Allah, lest you be thrown into the hellfire, blameworthy, rejected. (The Quran, chapter *The Night Journey*, 17:39).

This verse is the conclusion of multiple verses that precede it in which God expounded the fundamental principles of wisdom. It reinforces the fact that wisdom is indeed from God. This cautionary statement against ascribing partners to God is another way of impressing upon Muhammad, peace be upon him, the urgency of offering gratitude to the One and the Only One who has bestowed upon him this tremendous gift called wisdom. To impress upon us the magnitude of the blessing of wisdom, God says in chapter *The Cow*:

> He gives wisdom unto whom He pleases, and whosoever wisdom is given to, he indeed is given a lot of good, but none does remember except the people of the living heart. (The Quran, chapter *The Cow*, 2:269)

This verse, besides emphasizing the magnitude of the gift of wisdom, also makes it very clear for us that wisdom is a gift from God, and therefore, it is unattainable through any other means except by the will of God.

The two previous verses establish two facts about wisdom that are crucial to our understanding of its nature: 1. That wisdom is divine in origin, and therefore, only God can bestow it unto whoever He wills (*mashi'a*);

2. That the essence of gratitude (*shukr*) is to recognize the place from where one received the blessing and never to forget to recognize our gift by words or by actions. Ingratitude, on the other hand, is to ascribe that gift in part or entirely to any source other than the One it came from, thus making partners (*shirk*) with our true Benefactor. The letters which make the word *shirk* (sh-r-k) are the same letters which make the word *shukr* (sh-k-r). This makes clear the link between *shirk* (ingratitude) and its opposite, *shukr* (gratitude).

The purpose of this reminder about gratitude and a warning against ingratitude also explain that wisdom is not rigid nor static, but open to growth and expansion. The means to that growth and expansion is gratitude. Hence, Moses declares to his people:

> And when your Lord proclaimed, "If you offer gratitude I will give you increase, but if you are ungrateful, surely My punishment is formidable." (The Quran, chapter *Abraham*, 14:7)

Thus, one who receives wisdom from God must strive in offering gratitude and seeking for more wisdom.

In the story of Luqman the Wise, the first admonishment that God addressed unto him after granting him wisdom was to be grateful to God, the Bestower of wisdom. Thus, we read in Chapter *Luqman*:

> And We indeed gave wisdom unto Luqman saying, "Now do offer gratitude to Allah." Thus, whosoever offers gratitude [to Allah], he only offers gratitude for the good of his own soul, and whoever is ungrateful, truly Allah is Self-Sufficient, All Praiseworthy. (The Quran, chapter *Luqman*, 31:12)

Here, God impresses upon Luqman the fact that being grateful is only beneficial for one who is grateful, since there is no benefit that accrues to God from our gratitude. Further, the verse specifies that gratitude, in essence, constitutes two things: 1. *Ḥamd*: praise and glorification (God, however, is self-praised and self-glorified; therefore, our praise or glorification is simply in addition to His own); 2. *Ghinā*: God is Self-Sufficient; therefore, our offerings and charities, as well as our acts of devotion, avails Him in no way. This is further explained in chapter *The Pilgrimage*:

Their flesh never reaches Allah nor their blood [of their sacrifice], but the God-reverence from you reaches up to Him. Thus, He has made them subservient to you, so that you may extol the grandeur of Allah for the reason that He has guided you, and give glad tidings to the ones who act in excellence. (The Quran, chapter *The Pilgrimage*, 22:37)

God is Self-Praiseworthy and does not need our praises; He is Self-Sufficient and does not need our help, so the entire benefit is ours. This fact must be clear in our minds when we worship, lest we wrongly think that we are entitled to something from God by virtue of our worship, or that we can add or take away from God's glory and majesty when we worship Him (or when we do not).

And there is no grace for anyone in His presence to be paid with by way of entitlement; it is just a desire to seek the face of his Lord, The Most-High. (The Quran, chapter *The Night*, 92:19-20)

CHAPTER 9

Remembrance and Gratitude

Wisdom exists between remembrance on the one hand and gratitude on the other. In other words, wisdom is rooted in remembrance, and develops and grows outwardly through gratitude. In the first place, wisdom is given as a reward for one who establishes the remembrance of God, and thereafter through remembrance it continues to live. In the event of forgetfulness, it slowly disappears due to the fact that the heart has hardened up. In relationship to this point, God makes the following reference:

> Because of their violation of their solemn covenant, We cursed them and We made their hearts hard. They bias the word from its rightful disposition and they forgot a share from that which was given to them as a reminder, and you will continue to discover treachery from them except from a few among them, but pardon them and turn away in a nicely way. Truly Allah loves those who act in excellence. (The Quran, chapter *The Heavenly Food Bowl*, 5:13)

Thus, remembrance is both the origin and the maintainer of wisdom. This tight relationship between remembrance (*dhikr*) and wisdom (*ḥikma*) is so close that one is called by the name of the other.

With regards to David, God says:

> And We indeed wrote in the psalms after the remembrance that the earth, it will be inherited by My righteous servants. (The Quran, chapter *The Prophets*, 21:105)

Remembrance here means wisdom. In another place, the disbelievers contend that no wisdom was sent unto the Prophet, peace be upon him:

"Is the remembrance sent down on him from among us?" Nay, they are in incredulity about My remembrance. Nay! They have not yet tasted My punishment. (The Quran, chapter *Sad*, 38:8)

In a similar manner, the people of Thamud denied that the remembrance was sent down unto Salih:

"Has the remembrance been sent down on him [alone] from among us? Nay! He is a liar most arrogant." (The Quran, chapter *The Moon*, 54:25)

Thus, wisdom thrives between remembrance and gratitude, and one must follow the other in such a manner that whenever we are reminded of a blessing from God, we must quickly follow that remembrance with an act of gratitude.

Therefore remember Me and I will remember you, and be grateful to Me and do not be ungrateful to Me. (The Quran, chapter *The Cow*, 2:152)

This means that gratitude must follow on the heels of remembrance.

And it is He who has made the night and the day to alternate for such a one who wishes to remember Allah or seeks to offer gratitude. (The Quran, chapter *The Criterion*, 25:62)

Like in the example of the alternation between night and day, there must be alternation between remembrance and gratitude.

CHAPTER 10

Wisdom and Faith

A similar relationship, like that of remembrance and gratitude, exists between wisdom and faith. This fact is reported in a prophetic tradition (*hadīth*) mentioned by Bukhari, in his authentic collection of prophetic traditions, that Anas bin Malik, the companion of the Prophet, peace and blessings of God be upon him, said:

> "I heard the Prophet say, 'The night he was taken from the holy mosque of Kaaba (in Mecca), three people came to him — and that was before revelation came down to him — while he was asleep in the sanctuary of the Sacred Mosque. The first among them said, 'Where is he?' The middle person said, "He is the most outstanding among them.' The third person said, 'Then pick that one who is most outstanding among them.' That was all for that night.' He, peace be upon him, did not see them until they came to him another night, when his heart was awake, but his eyes were asleep. Similarly, the prophets, their eyes sleep, but their hearts sleep not. They did not speak a word to him, but rather they picked him up and they placed him beside the well of *zamzam*. Then, Gabriel (Jibril) took him over from them. He opened up his body between his groin to his neck and washed it with the water of *zamzam* until he was done with his chest and his insides. Then, a golden pitcher was brought, which was filled with faith and wisdom, and he emptied it into his bosom and entrails and the lower throat and then sealed up everything" (Bukhari).

This authentic narration clearly links faith with wisdom. The nature of the relationship between them is simply that of cause: wisdom is granted on the grounds that faith is secured first. Wisdom is rooted in faith and also made to thrive by it, in such a way that every increase in faith will reflect in an increase in wisdom.

Another very important aspect of this relationship is that both *īmān* (faith) and wisdom are concerned with the horizontal perception. In other words, they both relate to God's magnificence. The perception of magnificence relates to the horizontal balance plane called *ʿaql* (reason; rational intelligence). Thus, the point at which faith and wisdom were introduced into the heart and bosom of the Prophet, peace be upon him, was at his departure point through the horizontal plane, which began from the holy sanctuary in Mecca all the way to the holy sanctuary in Jerusalem (*Aqsa*).

When his horizontal journey came to an end and he had to travel vertically, then the perception switched from wisdom to knowledge and from faith to self-surrender. This switch was marked by the container of milk that was presented to the Prophet, peace be upon him, along with another jar containing wine. He chose the jar with milk and drank from it. Thereupon, Gabriel remarked, "You have chosen in accordance with the *fiṭra* (righteous disposition of Islam)" (Bukhari). The word *fiṭra* indicates that the context is one of *taslīm* (self-surrender), which is symbolized by milk. Milk is also interpreted as knowledge. The symbolic representation of knowledge by milk is mentioned in another prophetic narration, where the Prophet, peace be upon him, in a dream, was offered a jar of milk. He drank from it and passed the remainder to his companion, Umar. When asked what it meant, he said, "Knowledge" (Bukhari).

Thus, our awareness and perceptions are adjusted according to their appropriate contexts. If we are moving through a horizontal plane, then our perception should be adjusted accordingly, through the emphasis of wisdom. If we are travelling through a vertical plane, then our perception should be adjusted accordingly, which refers to knowledge.

The Fluctuation of Wisdom and Faith

As we notice from the aforementioned prophetic tradition with regards to the nightly journey, the Prophet, peace be upon him, underwent a thorough preparation before he started the journey. This preparation began by using the water of *zamzam* to purify both the inside and the outside of his body, peace be upon him, before introducing the substance of faith and wisdom into it. This substance also proves the significance of ritual purification, whether just the ablution or the ritual bath for it was only after the ritual purification that wisdom and faith were granted. This further indicates that wisdom and faith are subject to increase and decrease because by the time this incident took place, the Prophet, peace be upon him, had already received wisdom and faith since the inception of the revelation. Therefore, these two were only being replenished.

> He it is who sent down tranquility in the hearts of the believers so that they may increase in faith along with their faith, and for Allah are the hosts of the heavens and of the earth; truly Allah is All-knowing, All-wise. (The Quran, chapter *The Victory*, 48:4)

> And Allah will increase those who have attained to guidance in guidance. And the good deeds that remain are better in the sight of Your Lord as a reward and better as a place of return. (The Quran, chapter *Mary*, 19:76)

Thus, all blessings — including faith and wisdom — are open to increase, and this depends on gratitude.

> And when your Lord proclaimed, "If you offer gratitude, I will give you increase, but if you be ungrateful, surely My punishment is formidable." (The Quran, chapter *Abraham*, 14:7)

There is always an occasion which justifies this increase in faith and wisdom. It may be that the believer is about to face some new challenges in his or her life, or some new hurdles on his or her path, and therefore, God gives him or her this increase to fortify his or her heart and strengthen his or her resolve. In this case, the Prophet, peace be upon him, was about to embark on the journey that would take him across the various layers of the world — internal and external, horizontal and vertical — to the presence of his Lord. He had been prepared for this journey since he was six, and now the final moment had come for him to go and meet his Lord in the innermost precinct of His presence. For this reason, he did not ingest the supply of faith and wisdom unconsciously. Instead he underwent an outwardly physical operation, so that his heart, soul, and body could all be permeated with faith and wisdom. A similar phenomenon was to happen later when he would be offered a jar of milk and drank it until it exuded through his nose and ears.

CHAPTER 11

The Fruit of Faith and Wisdom

Later in the Prophet's journey, peace be upon him, the role of this increase in faith and wisdom became clear: to increase his heart in balance and steadiness. This increase, in turn, bore *its* fruit: *taqwa* (God-reverence). Thus, when God speaks of the provision for one's journey, he is referring to *taqwa*, which a traveller needs to keep on the straight path and not wander to the left nor the right. Without it, he or she is sure to be tempted off the path.

> The pilgrimage consists of months well marked so whoever takes upon himself the pilgrimage within these [months], then there should be no obscenity and no acts of renegation and no arguments in the pilgrimage. And whatever you do of good, Allah does know it, and carry with you your provision of the way. Lo! The best provision of the way indeed is the reverence of Allah, so revere Me, O people of the heart. (The Quran, chapter *The Cow*, 2:197)

Taqwa is the product of faith and wisdom, and any increase in these two leads to an increase in *taqwa*. *Taqwa*, in turn, brings coolness and joy to our eyes, our heart, and our soul, so that our heart and our gaze do not wander. The significance of arming oneself with wisdom and faith lies in the fact that the way is fraught with various types of distractions that may attract the gaze of the traveller and cause him to wander off his path. Thus, *taqwa* helps the traveller keep his faith strong on his mission; otherwise, he runs the risk of never making it to the destination, or if he does, missing the ultimate point of his journey. This is what God summed up in this verse:

The [Prophet Muhammad's] sight did not wander nor did it [the sight] transgress. (The Quran, chapter *The Star*, 53:17)

The Prophet's gaze, peace be upon him, did not wander because his heart was filled with reverence for God (*taqwa*) and his gaze did not exceed the limit (transgress) because his heart was filled with deference for God (*khashiya*). As a result, the ultimate point was reached:

> Truly he saw the most great from among the signs of his Lord. (The Quran, chapter *The Star*, 53:18)

Had his gaze wandered off by an inch or transgressed, then the ultimate point would have been missed.

The Role of Taqwa in Reaching One's Destination

There are a few authentic narrations that give us a glimpse into the nature of the challenges the Prophet, peace be upon him, faced on his way from the sacred mosque in Mecca to the holy mosque in Jerusalem. One narration that relates these challenges is reported by Bayhaqi from the companion Abu Sa'eed al Khudri that the Prophet, peace be upon him, said:

> While I was asleep at night in the holy mosque, someone came and woke me up and when I woke up, I saw no one. Thereafter, I saw a silhouette and I followed it with my gaze until I came out of the mosque. Thereupon, I saw a boat, which resembles this beast of yours: the zebra; it had drooping ears, called the *Burāq*. The prophets before me tried to ride on it. Its hoofs reach the distance of its gaze. I mounted on it, and while I was going, I heard a caller from my right side, 'O Muhammad, wait for me, I need to ask you.' I did not respond to him. While I was going again, a caller called me from my left side, 'O Muhammad, wait for me, I want to ask you;' again, I did not respond to him. I went on, and while I was going, I saw a female figure with bare arms and she was decked with all kinds of ornaments ever created by God and she said, 'O Muhammad! Wait for me, I want to ask you.' I did not pay heed to her and I did not wait for her until I reached Jerusalem. Then, I was presented with a jug of wine and a jug of milk. I drank the milk and I left the wine and Gabriel said, 'You have indeed found the *fitra*.' I acclaimed, God is great (twice). Gabriel said, 'What did you encounter on your way here?' I said, 'While I was going, a

caller called me from the right, 'O Muhammad, wait for me, let me ask you,' but I did not respond to him and I did not wait for him either.' He (Gabriel) said, 'That is the caller unto Judaism; had you responded to him, then surely your nation would become Judaists.' I said, 'Then I was going when a caller called me from my left, saying, 'O Muhammad, wait for me, let me ask you.' I did not pay heed to him nor did I wait for him. He (Gabriel) said, 'That is the caller to Christianity; had your responded to him, then your nation would surely become Christians.' Furthermore, while I was going, I beheld a female figure with bare arms decked with every kind of ornament ever made by God, saying, 'O Muhammad, wait for me, let me ask you,' but I did not respond to her nor did I wait for her. He (Gabriel) said, 'That is the worldly life; had you responded to her, then your nation would surely choose the life of this world over the life of the hereafter.' (Bayhaqi, Ibn Kathir).

As we see from the narration quoted above, the path of the traveller is fraught with callers from the right, and the left, as well as from behind and from in front, and he is very susceptible to incline to them unless he is equipped with faith and wisdom (and their product, *taqwa*) which keeps his heart steady, upright, and focused on the purpose of his journey: the face of God and the life of the hereafter.

The straight path that leads to God is fraught with numerous challenges and temptations, ranging from those who are calling to biased faith, whether to the right or to the left, and those who are calling to the ornaments of this worldly life, which consists of spouses, wealth and children. The female figure at the end represented all three in one: spouse, children, and wealth. Hence, we see how God prepared the Prophet, peace be upon him, and armed him with fresh faith and wisdom to overcome these three major hurdles on the path of God. He did not respond to any of the three callers until he reached his destination, horizontally speaking (Jerusalem). His victory over these obstacles was celebrated by God in the following words:

The [Prophet Muhammad's] sight did not wander nor did it [the sight] transgress. Truly he saw the greatest from among the signs of his Lord. (The Quran, chapter *The Star*, 53:17-18)

Before this event, God had always admonished the Prophet, peace be upon him, to be content with that which He had bestowed upon him, and not extend his gaze unto what He had bestowed upon others:

> And do not stretch your gaze to that which We have granted as a temporary enjoyment to certain kinds of them and do not grieve over them and lower your wings for the believers. (The Quran, chapter *The Rocky Mountain*, 15:88)

> And keep yourself patient along with those who call their Lord in the morning and in the evening and they seek His face and do not let your eyes look past them, that you seek the adornment of the life of this world, and do not obey one whose heart We have caused to be oblivious about Our remembrance and he follows his vain desires and his affair has gone beyond redemption. (The Quran, chapter *The Cave*, 18:28)

> Wealth and children are adornment of the life of this world. But the things that are righteous and sustaining are better in reward in the sight of your Lord and are better in hope. (The Quran, chapter *The Cave*, 18:46)

These admonishments make it clear that the wealth we seek as our provision and the spouses and children that we seek as our garment and ornaments are all perishable. The best provision is *taqwa* (wisdom and faith) and the best garment and ornament is *taqwa*. Thus, once we have cultivated wisdom and faith, that results in God-reverence, God grants us from His quality of magnificence his endowments:

1. The provision of *taqwa*: that stems from God's Self-Sufficiency which endows us with an auto-sufficiency that lies as an inexhaustible treasure within one's heart so that he or she become needy of no one.

2. The dress of *taqwa*: in this, God invests (dons) us with a dress from His own dress of magnificence ("Magnificence is My cloak") which combines beauty and awesomeness (*hayba*).

Both the dress and the provision are placed within the heart of the believer:

> And know that among you is the messenger of Allah. If he were to obey you in many of the matters, you would certainly become stub-

born, but Allah has caused you to love the faith and has adorned it
[the faith] in your hearts and He caused you to abhor the disbelief
and the renegation and the disobedience. Those are the ones who
are well-guided [to the way]. (The Quran, chapter *The Inner Apartments*, 49:7)

The adornment of faith in the heart refers to its sweetness and
beauty. This internal adornment is what, in sum, means *taqwa* (God-reverence). The inward look at the adornments of faith in the heart offsets the
outward attractions of the ornaments of life of this world. The heart of the
believer is therefore at a crossroad between the love of faith, which draws
him towards the inner life of the hereafter, and the love of lust, which draws
him towards the outer life of this world. The significance of God-reverence
lies in the fact that it lends sweetness and beauty to faith which exercises a
greater pull towards the inner life of the hereafter. God says:

They only know the outer life of this world, but they are oblivious
of the hereafter [which is the inner life]. (The Quran, chapter *The
Romans*, 30:7)

Stations on the Way

In light of the Prophet's nightly journey, peace be upon him,
from Mecca to Jerusalem, we saw how the fresh dose of faith and wisdom
strengthened him further against the various temptations that sought to
draw his attention to the embellishments of the outer life of this world. His
gaze was turned completely inward until he reached where he needed to be.

However, since the journey to the Lord of the throne is daunting
and arduous, the traveller needs to pull in at stations on the way to replenish
his faith and wisdom, if the journey requires further horizontal travelling,
or replenish his God-deference (*khashiya*) for travelling vertically. Thus,
Mecca was his point of departure and Jerusalem was a station on the way.
At that station, the Prophet, peace be upon him, was offered different types
of substances from which he chose milk and drank it in preparation for the
second phase of his journey: the vertical ascension. Gabriel commented
with approval, "You have chosen in accordance with the *fitra* (righteous
disposition of Islam)" (Bukhari). For as milk nourishes the newly-born
infant and prepares him or her to be able to eat solid food after two years,
similarly the milk here prepares the person who drinks it to gain knowledge

from God, *without* mediation (*ladunni*) or *through* mediation (*khabari*).

It must be noted, however, that the milk is not knowledge in itself, but it rather prepares the drinker to receive knowledge. Likewise, the content of the golden pitcher introduced at the beginning of his journey – the substance of faith and wisdom – plays a similar role. There is a marked distinction between the person who drinks the milk before receiving knowledge and the person who does not. The former will have certainty with his knowledge, but the latter will not.

CHAPTER 12

Inheriting Knowledge and Wisdom

It is a matter of fact in the world of spirituality that every seeker must follow the footsteps of those who have gone before him on the path. This means that he will inherit the sum of their spiritual experiences (secrets, *asrār*) and then, if possible, move beyond them. Thus, the Prophet's night journey from Mecca to Jerusalem and then his ascension through the layers of the heavens was also that which can be qualified as an "educational journey" in the pursuit of gnosis. In this way, the gifts of those who preceded him are recognized as all proceeding from God:

> And in their wake, We sent Jesus son of Mary testifying to that which went before him from the Torah and We gave him the Gospel; in it, there is a guidance and a light testifying to that which went before it from the Torah and as a guidance and as an admonition for those who guard their own souls. (The Quran, chapter *The Heavenly Food Bowl*, 5:46)

> Then We sent unto you the book by the truth testifying to that which went before it from the book and superseding above it. Therefore judge between them by that which Allah has sent down and do not follow their vain desires, departing from that which has come to you from the truth. For each one of you, We have appointed a law and a way, and had Allah so willed, He certainly would have made you one nation, but it is that He may try you through that which He has given you; therefore, vie with one another in the good things. Unto Allah is your place of returning altogether and then He will inform you about all that wherein you used to disagree. (The Qu-

ran, chapter *The Heavenly Food Bowl*, 5:48)

Thus, the latter prophet confirms the former, and both are recognized as coming from one source:

And do not dispute with the people of the book except through that which is most excellent apart from those who among them have wronged their own souls and say, "We believe in that which has been sent down to us and which has been sent down to you and our God and your God is one but we have submitted to Him." (The Quran, chapter *The Spider*, 29:46)

The Advice of the Prophets

As the Prophet, peace be upon him, travelled that night, he encountered the prophets who came before him twice: the first time during the horizontal journey and the second time during the vertical journey. In the horizontal encounter, he received from them the wisdom which God had bestowed upon them, while in the vertical encounter, he received knowledge of the book. The tradition narrated by Baihaqi from Abu Hurayra gives a full detail of these encounters, but parts of it are also narrated by Bukhari, Muslim, Ahmad, etc. (See the book of 'Alawi al-Maliki on *'Isrā' wal-Mi'rāj: Prophet's Night Journey & Heavenly Ascent*).

His journey had two major objectives: to receive the trusts in the form of knowledge and wisdom, which had been placed in the care of the various prophets who had preceded him. God had taken a solemn vow from these prophets that if one day they encountered the Prophet, peace be upon him, they would believe in him and help him. Their belief in him and their help for him consisted in passing their knowledge and wisdom to him which was exactly what they did on that night:

And when Allah took the covenant of the prophets [saying] by virtue of that which I have given you in book and wisdom then comes to you a messenger confirming that which is with you, then certainly you must believe in him and you must certainly assist him. He said, "Do you agree and take on My firm pledge." They said, "Yes we agree," and He said, "Then bear witness and I am with you among the witnesses." (The Quran, chapter *The Family of Imran*, 3:81)

The Advice of Moses

Thus, by virtue of this covenant, the prophets he encountered passed onto him whatever trust God had given them and made available to him whatever assistance they were able to offer. This fact was nowhere more apparent than in the course of the Prophet's encounter with Moses, peace be upon them. In various authentic narrations by Bukhari and Muslim, by Abu Hatim in his commentary, Ahmad in his Musnad, and Baihaqi in Dalail they all narrate that when the Prophet Muhammad, peace be upon him, passed by Moses on his way after meeting with God, Moses, asked him, "What has your Lord prescribed upon you and your nation?" The Prophet, peace be upon him, replied, "Fifty prayers." Then Moses said to him, "Go back and ask your Lord to reduce it for you. Your nation cannot bear such a load. I have had my experience with people before you who were stronger than your nation and they were unable to carry such a load."

At the behest of Moses, he returned to God asking Him for reduction. Then, God reduced it by ten, or in some narrations by five. But Moses continued to send him back each time he came back from God until God reduced the prayers to five. This encounter with Moses is a resounding example of how godly people bear no grudge or hatred or animosity towards one another and that they do not hold back any type of assistance they can offer. By this advice, Moses rendered a great service to Prophet Muhammad, peace be upon him, and his nation at large.

The Historical Context of the Prophet's Night Journey

The nightly journey of the Prophet, peace be upon him, could not have come at a better time. It took place at a crucial juncture in his life and in his mission. Prior to this journey, both Khadijah, his wife, and Abu Talib, his uncle, had died. These two were the most important helpers and protectors for him. Following their death, he felt unprotected in Mecca, so he went to Taif, seeking help and a platform for his mission, but he was met with the most unwelcoming treatment he could possibly ever imagine. Against the background of these events, God summoned him to His Presence.

His journey also set the stage for his migration to Medina and the establishment of the Muslim community there. It took place at the end of the Meccan period and the commencement of the Medinan period, a time when the experiences of the prophets who preceded him could be most useful as he endeavored to carve out a Muslim state in the midst of the chaos that reigned in Arabia. From the minarets of the mosque of the Prophet, peace be upon him, in Medina went forth the call that would awaken the world from its long overdue slumber.

CHAPTER 13

Recognition and Wisdom

One of the most important aspects of wisdom is *ma'rifa*. It means to recognize God's blessings as God's blessings and not to deny them after recognizing them:

> They recognize the blessing of Allah, but then they deny it, and most of them are ungrateful. (The Quran, chapter *The Bee*, 16:83)

To recognize is to be aware of the fact that the blessings we enjoy indeed come from God and therefore must be treated with such regard as fitting of the gifts given from such an exalted King, the Almighty. People, therefore, fall into two categories: 1. Those who recognize God's blessings as from God and therefore give due regard and treat them with the utmost care; 2. Those who recognize God's blessings as such, but then disregard them, and treat them slightly. In the case of the former group, the blessings continue to grow and multiply, while in the case of the latter group, the blessings are turned into tribulations:

> Have you not seen those who have changed the blessing of Allah into ingratitude and caused their people to dwell in the home of perdition? (The Quran, chapter *Abraham*, 14:28)

> And whatever good is happening to you is from Allah, but then whenever harm touches you, surely it is to Him that you flee for help. (The Quran, chapter *The Bee*, 16:53)

> That is because Allah is never going to change a blessing that He has bestowed on a people until they change what is in their souls and truly Allah is All-hearing, All-knowing. (The Quran, chapter *The Gains of War*, 8:53)

Before him and behind him are angels who take turns. They protect him from the commandment of Allah. Allah does not change the state of a people until they change the state of their souls, and when Allah wills to bring harm to a people, there is none who can turn it away. They will have no one to be an ally for them besides Him. (The Quran, chapter *The Thunder*, 13:11)

The transfiguration referred to in this verse is regarding the alienation of what is right by alienating God's right. The way in which one alienates God's right is by failing to appreciate Him to His true appreciation:

And they have not evaluated Allah to His true worth. The earth altogether will be in His fist on the day of resurrection and the heavens will be rolled up like a scroll by His right hand. Glory be unto Him and far exalted is He above all that they ascribe as partners unto Him. (The Quran, chapter *The Flocks*, 39:67)

Thus, true appreciation leads to true recognition of God's right in full: to worship Him as He deserves, and to treat Him with reverence as He deserves. It is here that recognition (*ma'rifa*) meets reverence (*taqwa*), for anyone who recognizes God's worth to His true recognition must perforce revere Him with true reverence:

So it is that whoever reveres the insignia of Allah, that truly comes from the reverence of Allah that is in the hearts. (The Quran, chapter *The Pilgrimage*, 22:32)

Here, the recognition of God's magnificent worth is connected with reverence of the heart. This connection is highlighted elsewhere in chapter *The Inner Apartments*:

O you mankind! Truly We have created you from a male and a female and We have made you into nations and tribes so that you may recognize one another. Truly the most graceful among you in the sight of Allah is one who reveres Him the most. Truly Allah is All-knowing, All-acquainted. (The Quran, chapter *The Inner Apartments*, 49:13)

God clearly states the reason why He chose to divide up humanity into various segments (nations, tribes, clans, etc.): to facilitate for us to recognize our blood ties according to the degrees of closeness. By recognizing the degrees in blood relation, we ascribe to each and everyone what is their right. To recognize and appreciate the right of the kin is part and parcel of appreciating and recognizing the right of God starting with the closest: the parents, the children, the siblings, etc. In the end of the verse, He impresses upon our minds the inseparability between His right and the blood right, "Truly the most graceful among you in the sight of Allah is one who reveres Him the most." (The Quran, chapter *The Inner Apartments*, 49:13). The most honoured is one who recognizes both rights with true recognition:

> O you humankind! Revere your Lord who created you from one soul and created from it its pair and disseminated from both of them many men and women, and revere Allah by Whom you ask one another and [revere] the blood ties. Truly Allah is indeed All-watchful over you. (The Quran, chapter *The Women*, 4:1)

Taqwa, "reverence" in the imperative form, is repeated three times in this verse: 1. To revere your Lord who created you from one soul; 2. To revere God in whose name you make your claims (to your rights); and 3. To revere your blood ties. These triple commands entail the recognition of God's right as the sole Creator; then the recognition of every individual life as an essential of the one life that was first created, and then recognition of the right of the near of kin. Anyone who recognizes these three rights with full recognition is surely the one most honoured in the sight of God.

PART III

THE WISDOM OF THE PROPHET MUHAMMAD
PEACE BE UPON HIM

CHAPTER 14

The 1ˢᵗ Principle: The Right of God

The seven principles of wisdom were discussed earlier in Part I, entitled "The Wisdom of Luqman" (from chapter *Luqman*). These principles, in essence, are always the same, differing only in terms of details. These ones now under discussion are entitled, "The Wisdom of Muhammad, peace be upon him," as stated in the following verse:

> That is part of what your Lord has revealed unto you from the wisdom, and do not make with Allah another deity lest you will be thrown in hellfire, blameworthy and banished. (The Quran, chapter *The Night Journey*, 17:39)

The seven principles are expounded in much more detail here than in Chapter *Luqman*.

The first principle, like in Chapter *Luqman*, is concerned with recognizing the right of God with full recognition. This full recognition leads into the true reverence, which is the essence of worship:

> And your Lord has ordained that you should worship none except Him and [He has also ordained] kindness to parents. If one or both of them attain old age with you, do not tell them 'fie' and do not treat them uncouthly and do speak to them with a gracious speech. (The Quran, chapter *The Night Journey*, 17:23)

True reverence (*ḥaqq al taqwa*) or true worship is the means by which God's Magnificence (*'aẓamah*) is truly appreciated. The ultimate purpose of our existence consists of truly appreciating God's Magnificence in order to find the meaning of love:

> Except those whom you have made covenant with from among those who ascribe partners to Allah and thereafter they have not cheated you anything in the least and they have not backed anyone against you so fulfill the covenant for them until its term. Truly Allah loves those who guard their own souls. (The Quran, chapter *The Repentance*, 9:4)

> How could there be any covenant in the sight of Allah and in the sight of His messenger for those who ascribe partners to Allah except the ones with whom you have made the covenant in the precinct of the sacred mosque. Therefore as long as they observe their duty to you, then do observe your duty to them. Truly Allah loves those who safeguard their own souls. (The Quran, chapter *The Repentance*, 9:7)

> Nay! Indeed whoever fulfills his firm pledge and safeguards his own soul, then truly Allah loves those who safeguard their own souls. (The Quran, chapter *The Family of Imran*, 3:76)

Love, therefore, is the fruit of true appreciation of God's Magnificence, followed by true reverence for Him:

> O you who believe! Revere Allah His true reverence and you should not die except that you are in submission [to Him]. (The Quran, chapter *The Family of Imran*, 3:102)

This reverence for God, according to a prophetic tradition, consists of three things: 1. To remember Him and not forget Him; 2. To be grateful to Him and not be ungrateful; 3. To obey Him and not disobey Him. Together, these three amount to actual appreciation of God's Magnificence and true reverence for Him, earning the worshipper the Love of God:

> And I have not created the Jinns and the humankind except that they serve Me [in truth]. (The Quran, chapter *The Scatterers*, 51:56)

According to the interpretation of Ibn Abbas, may God be pleased with him, "serve Me" here means to recognize God's true Worth and Magnificence.

CHAPTER 15

The 2ⁿᵈ Principle: The Right of Parents

The second principle consists of recognizing the rights of parents. Their right as parents stem from the right of God. God created you, and your parents earned you (*kasb*); in a prophetic tradition, the Prophet, peace be upon him, said, "Your children are from your earnings." In consequence, their right has the same triple ramifications as that of God's: remembrance, gratitude, and obedience.

Remembrance

To remember one's parents entails invoking God's mercy and forgiveness for them, while also showing tenderness and humility towards them:

> And your Lord has ordained that you should worship none except Him and [He has also ordained] kindness to parents. If one or both of them attain old age with you, do not tell them 'fie' and do not treat them uncouthly and do speak to them with a gracious speech and out of mercy, spread for them the wings of tenderness and humility and say, "O my Lord, bestow [Your] mercy on both of them, as they raised me when I was small." (The Quran, chapter *The Night Journey*, 17:23-24)

Abraham, peace be upon him, prayed for his parents:

> And cover my father with forgiveness, as he indeed is of those gone astray. (The Quran, chapter *The Poets*, 26:86)

In chapter *The Cow*, God joins His remembrance with the remembrance of the parents:

> And when you have completed your rituals, then remember Allah as much as you remember your parents or an even greater remembrance. And among mankind are those who say, "O our Lord, give us in this life" and there is no portion for him in the hereafter. (The Quran, chapter *The Cow*, 2:200)

Gratitude

Gratitude means any act that pleases your parents and makes them content and brings them coolness of the eye to the point that they never wish they had any other child:

> And those who say, "O our Lord, grant unto us from our spouses and our children such as are coolness of eyes and make us leaders for those who safeguard their own souls." (The Quran, chapter *The Criterion*, 25:74)

That coolness of the eye consists of never causing any grief to your parents, which is also knowns as "kindness to the parents" (*birr al wālidayn*). Both John (Yahya) and Jesus (Isa), peace be upon them, even though they were prophets, counted kindness to parents among their virtues:

> O Yahya! Hold the book with all your strength and We had given him the wisdom while still a child. And [he was granted] tenderness from Our presence and purity and he was reverent to Allah. And kind to his parents and never was he overbearing, disobedient. And peace be upon him the day he was born and the day he dies and the day he will be raised alive. (The Quran, chapter *Mary*, 19:12-15)

As for Jesus and his mother, God says that Jesus said the following:

> He said, "I am a slave of Allah and He has given me the book and He has made me a prophet and He has made me blessed wheresoever I may be and He has admonished me to prayer and to self-purification as long as I am alive and He has made me kind to my mother and has not made me overbearing, miserable and [the greeting of] peace was on me the day I was born and the day that I die and the day that I will be raised a living." (The Quran, chapter *Mary*, 19:30-

33)

About the mother of Moses, God says the following:

> So We returned him to his mother so that her eye may find coolness
> of the eye and that she may not grieve and that she may know that
> the promise of Allah is true, but most of them do not know. (The
> Quran, chapter *The Stories*, 28:13)

Furthermore, in chapter *Luqman*, God joins gratitude towards Him with
gratitude towards the parents:

> And We have exhorted the human being regarding his parents. His
> mother carried him in weakness upon weakness and his weaning is
> in two years. So offer gratitude to Me and to your parents, unto Me
> is the place of final coming. (The Quran, chapter *Luqman*, 31:14)

Gratitude towards God or towards the parents means doing what pleases
them:

> If you show ingratitude, truly Allah is All-self-sufficient from you,
> but He does not please the ingratitude for His slaves. But if you are
> grateful, He is pleased with it for your sake and no bearer of a bur-
> den can bear the burden of another and then unto your Lord will
> be your place of return. Then He will inform you about all that you
> used to do. Truly He is All-knowing about the essence of the bo-
> soms. (The Quran, chapter *The Flocks*, 39:7)

The relationship between gratitude and good pleasure (*riḍwān*) is further
elucidated by the following verse:

> And when your Lord proclaimed, "If you offer gratitude, I will give
> you increase, but if you be ungrateful, surely My punishment is for-
> midable." (The Quran, chapter *Abraham*, 14:7)

The increase mentioned in this verse is in reference to the good pleasure of
God, for anything that receives God's pleasure is bound for an open-ended
increase and expansion:

> For those who act in excellence is the reward of excellence and in-

crease. And their faces are neither afflicted by weariness nor by humiliation. Those are the companions of the paradise and they will abide therein forever. (The Quran, chapter *Jonah*, 10:26)

In sum, gratitude from the servant is rewarded with increase from God and that increase is God's good pleasure.

Obedience

The third ramification of the right of the parents is to obey them as far as it does not clash with obedience to God:

If you ever do turn away from them in pursuit of a mercy from your Lord which you expect, then speak to them a word of ease and gentleness. (The Quran, chapter *The Night Journey*, 17:28)

Thus, the pursuit of God's mercy takes precedence over obedience to the parents, and that includes any type of pursuit that contributes towards the fulfillment of one's word:

And We have enjoined unto mankind that he should be kind to his parents, but if they force you to ascribe as a partner to Me such a thing about which you have no knowledge, then obey them not. Your place of return is unto Me and then I will inform you about all that you used to do. (The Quran, chapter *The Spider*, 29:8)

Similarly, in chapter *Luqman*, God says:

But if they [your parents] urge you to ascribe such things as partners to Me for which you have no knowledge, then obey them not, but keep them a goodly company in this world and follow the way of one who has turned back to Me. Then unto Me will be your place of return and then I will inform you about all that you used to do. (The Quran, chapter *Luqman*, 31:15)

The word "obey" here is synonymous with following, and God is clearly saying that you should not follow your parents in matters they have no knowledge about because you only follow one who knows; it is dangerous to follow someone who does not know:

O my father, something from the knowledge has indeed come to me that has not come to you, therefore follow me and I will guide you to a way which is midmost. (The Quran, chapter *Mary*, 19:43)

Therefore, in terms of leadership and guidance, parents do not count unless they are people of knowledge, for only one who knows must be followed, and this is replicated by the verse in chapter *Luqman*:

But if they [your parents] urge you to ascribe such things as partners to Me for which you have no knowledge, then obey them not, but keep them a goodly company in this world and follow the way of one who has turned back to Me. Then unto Me will be your place of return and then I will inform you about all that you used to do. (The Quran, chapter *Luqman*, 31:15)

The one who has reverted to God is the one who is endowed with knowledge. To highlight the dangers of following one who does not know, God equates doing so with ascribing partners to God, which is the most heinous wrongdoing:

And when Luqman said to his son while he admonished him, "O my son! Do not ascribe partners to Allah. Truly ascribing partners to Allah is an egregious wrongdoing." (The Quran, chapter *Luqman*, 31:13)

It amounts to associating partners with God (*shirk*) to seek to please parents (*shukr*) in something that is not their right. On the contrary, God has admonished us to inquire from people of remembrance:

And We did not send anyone before you except men unto whom We sent Our inspiration, so ask the people of remembrance if you do not know. (The Quran, chapter *The Bee*, 16:43)

And He has also admonished us to obey the people of command:

O you who believe! Obey Allah and obey the messenger and the people of the commandment among you. But if you disagree about anything, then refer it back to Allah and to the messenger if you indeed believe in Allah and in the last day. That is better and most excellent in interpretation. (The Quran, chapter *The Women*, 4:59)

CHAPTER 16

The 3rd Principle: The Right of One's Soul

T he former two principles concern our relationship with those whose actions resulted in our coming into existence: God who created us and our parents who earned us (in reference to the *ḥadīth*: "Your children are from your earnings"). The following principles are all centered around the soul (*nafs*), its right to what it earns and about others who are entitled to those earnings.

These earnings consist principally of two things: children and wealth. Since children and wealth are the twin earnings of the soul, children are the most entitled to our wealth, but they are not the only ones. The kinsfolk, the needy, and the wayfarer also all have their share in it among others. However, our gains and the manner of their distribution are part of our efforts towards social reform. The most important feature of this third principle of wisdom is self-reform, which takes precedence over social reform. This self-reform fundamentally consists of exhorting our own soul to embrace righteousness and to eschew all forms of wrongfulness. The task of disciplining one's own soul is a formidable task, since God says that Prophet Joseph (Yusuf), peace be upon him, said:

> And I do not claim my soul to be innocent. Indeed the soul does prompt to what is evil except that which my Lord has graced with His mercy. My Lord indeed is Oft-Forgiving, All-merciful. (The Quran, chapter *Joseph*, 12:53)

It is therefore imprudent to glorify one's own soul by taking it as an authority in every matter without verification. Contrary to the common legal tenet that everyone is innocent until proven guilty, it is proposed that everyone should say to themselves: my soul is guilty until proven innocent. It was with this in mind that Prophet Joseph, peace be upon him, made the above statement (12:53). The reformation of the soul, therefore, entails bringing the soul from the state of guilt to the state of innocence, and this process is known as growing the soul (*tazkiya al nafs*), as opposed to stunting the soul (*dass al nafs*). This growing or stunting is a matter of choice since every soul is offered the two means: the means for growing and the means for stunting. The means for growing the soul is the good word:

> Have you not seen how Allah sets forth the parable of a goodly word, which is like a goodly tree. Its root is firmly established [in the earth] and its branches [extending] into the heaven. Bringing forth its fruit in every season by the permission of its Lord, and Allah sets parables for the human beings so that they may remember. (The Quran, chapter *Abraham*, 14:24-5)

> Whoever is seeking the might, truly all the might is for Allah. To Him mounts up the good word, and the good deed He raises it up. And those who are scheming the evil deeds, for them is a formidable punishment and the scheme of this, it is this that is going to waste. (The Quran, chapter *Originator of Creation*, 35:10)

This good word is usually identified by the word *taqwa* (God-reverence) and called the *word of taqwa*. On the other hand, the means for stunting the soul is the *evil word*:

> And the likeness of an evil word is like that of an evil tree which is uprooted unto the surface of the earth having no place to settle in. (The Quran, chapter *Abraham*, 14:26)

The evil word is also identified as the word of transgression (*al fūjūr*):

> And by a soul and how He extended its creation. And then He inspired it to know its transgression and its self-guard. Indeed he is prospered, one who has sanctified it. And indeed he is lost, one who has stunted it. (The Quran, chapter *The Sun*, 91:7-10)

God-reverence as the means of growing the soul comprises of three disciplines, and it is through the application of these three disciplines that the soul grows strong and firm from without, but tender and gentle from within:

> Muhammad, messenger of Allah, and those with him are firm
> against the disbelievers, merciful among themselves. You see them
> bowing and prostrating; they seek favor from Allah and pleasure.
> Their marks are in their faces from the trace of prostration. That is
> their similitude in the Torah, and their similitude in the gospel is
> like a plant which sends forth its shoot and then it supported it and
> then it grew stout and then it rose up straight on its stalk. It caused
> the farmers to marvel so that He causes the disbelievers to enrage
> by them. Allah promises those who believed and did righteous
> deeds from among them a forgiveness and a most magnificent re-
> ward. (The Quran, chapter *The Victory*, 48:29)

These three disciplines are: 1. The discipline of remembrance of God; 2.
The discipline of gratitude; 3. The discipline of obedience. The concerted
application of these three disciplines empowers the word of God-reverence
within the soul, and as the word grows, the souls grows with it until the
word is fulfilled and the soul has attained its full potential.

Conversely, the word of transgression consists of three constitu-
ents, namely: 1. Forgetfulness; 2. Ingratitude; 3. Disobedience. As one continues to indulge in these three practices, the soul gets stunted further and
further, internally and externally.

> And know that among you is the messenger of Allah. If he were to
> obey you in many of the matters, you will certainly become stub-
> born, but Allah has caused you to love the faith and has adorned it
> [the faith] in your hearts and He caused you to abhor the disbelief
> and the renegation and the disobedience. Those are the ones who
> are well-guided [to the way]. (The Quran, chapter *The Inner Apart-
> ments*, 49:7)

Prayer and Patience

God, the All-Merciful, has however not abandoned us to fend for
ourselves, and has offered us help if we seek it from Him in the right manner. That right approach consists of two aspects: 1. Steadfastness in prayer
and 2. Patience. With this right approach, one can secure God's help to bear
the weighty word of God-reverence (*taqwa*), as God says:

And seek help through patience and prayer, and truly it is surely hard except on those who are humble. Who expect that they are going to meet their Lord and that they indeed are going to return to Him. (The Quran, chapter *The Cow*, 2:45-46)

O you who believe! Seek help through patience and prayer. Truly Allah is with those who are patient. (The Quran, chapter *The Cow*, 2:153)

And command your family to the prayer and be steadfast on it. We do not charge you with providing [for yourself and for them]. We provide for you and the good ending is for those who revere Allah. (The Quran, chapter *Taha*, 20:132)

Lord of the heavens and of the earth and what is between the two, therefore worship Him and be patient in worshipping Him. Do you know of any namesake for Him? (The Quran, chapter *Mary*, 19:65)

Thus, steadfastness in prayer and patience in the face of trials and tribulations are indispensable requirements for the reformation of the soul and the attainment of God-reverence. The Prophet, peace be upon him, said in his supplication: "O Allah, assist me to remember You, to be grateful to You, and to excellent in worshipping You (obeying You)." In another supplication, he said: "O Allah, grant my soul its God-reverence, You are its master and caretaker, and make it grow; You are the One who is best in making it grow."

Similarly, Luqman in his instructions to his son as he taught him wisdom, advised him to be steadfast in prayer and to be patient in order to reform his own self before embarking on reforming others:

O my son! Establish the prayer and command unto kindness and forbid from meanness and bear with patience whatever happens to you. Truly that is among the most resolute of all the affairs. (The Quran, chapter *Luqman*, 31:17)

In the sister chapters, *The One Wrapped* and *The One Wrapped in Cloak*, God urges the Prophet Muhammad, peace be upon him, to embark on the mission of social reform first through patience and prayer:

O you the one wrapped. Stand [for the prayer] through the night except for a little; half of it or make it a little less than that. Or make it more than that and recite the Quran with a careful recitation. We indeed are soon going to deliver unto you a heavy word. Truly the growing hours of the night are greater in impact and most upright in speech. Truly in the day there is for you a lengthy course of adoration. And remember the name of your Lord and devote yourself to Him with a whole devotion; Lord of the East and of the West. There is no deity except He, therefore take Him as a trustee. And bear with patience all that they say and forsake them with a nicely forsaking. (The Quran, chapter *The One Wrapped*, 73:1-10)

Patience and prayer come before embarking on the mission of social reform:

O you the one wrapped in cloak. Rise up and warn. And your Lord! Do proclaim His greatness. And your garment, keep it clean. And the abominations, do forsake. And do not boast about your gifts in order to seek aggrandizement for yourself. And for your Lord, be patient. But when the trumpet will sound. Then that day indeed is a most difficult day. For disbelievers it is not easy at all. (The Quran, chapter *The One Wrapped in Cloak*, 74:1-10)

CHAPTER 17

The 4th Principle: The Right of Society Via Wealth

The fourth principle represent different aspects of the third
principle — the right of the soul — with regards to different contexts.

Your Lord knows well what is within your souls. If you be righteous
[within your souls], then He indeed is Oft-Forgiving for those who
are criers unto Him. (The Quran, chapter *The Night Journey*, 17:25)

After speaking of the reform of the soul, God speaks about social reform by
order of priority:

And give unto the near of kin what is due to him and unto the
needy and unto the wayfarer and do not squander extravagantly.
(The Quran, chapter *The Night Journey*, 17:26)

God urges giving to those who have a right in our wealth and
warns against squandering it. These admonitions are in keeping with the
understanding that wealth belongs to God and that we are simply managers
in His name. We have no right to squander it, which if we do, we are surely
depriving those who are entitled to it by their rights:

Believe in Allah and in His messenger and spend from that in which
He made you vicegerents and as for those who believe from among
you and spend, for them there is a great reward. (The Quran, chapter *The Iron*, 57:7)

The judicious management of the resources that God has put at our disposal is the central feature of this principle. It is part of wisdom to realize that the inequality between people with regards to material possession is not a sign of grace or disgrace from God, but rather the result of a higher wisdom only known to God. However, empathy with those whose provisions are constricted should not compel us to disregard the right of our own soul and that of our immediate dependents.

> And do not tie your hand to your neck [out of stinginess] and do not stretch it out completely or you will be sitting down blameworthy weary. Indeed your Lord expands the sustenance for whom He wills and constricts [to whom He wills]. Truly He is All-acquainted, All-seeing about His slaves.(The Quran, chapter *The Night Journey*, 17:29-30)

These verses are clearly showing that there are times to take when it is right to take, and other times to give when it is right to give. Thus, knowing that the conditions of His servants reflects the workings of God's names: the One Who Contracts (*Al Qābiḍ*) and the One Who Expands (*Al Bāṣiṭ*).

The case of the orphans and the management of their properties is maintained separately from the needy and the wayfarer, even though they are commonly grouped together in the Quran as a way of highlighting the gravity of any offense towards them. The social consequences of any wrong towards them is equal to the social consequences of adultery; thus:

> And do not come near to adultery. It indeed is an act of injustice and an evil way. (The Quran, chapter *The Night Journey*, 17:32)

> And do not come near the property of the orphan except by way of goodness until he reaches the fullness of his strength, and fulfill the promise, for the promise is certainly going to be questioned about. (The Quran, chapter *The Night Journey*, 17:34)

This extra emphasis against adultery and consuming the property of an orphan is due to the fact that they entail a compound crime which carries a compound sin. The compound crime is the premeditation of the sin, which entails the formulation of an evil intent, and the execution of that intent, both of which are sins.

The 5th Principle: The Right of Society Via Progeny

This principle, the right of progeny, is the twin principle to the former. The preservation of progeny is a key component of social reform because progeny and wealth are the twin gains of the soul. Important social transactions, such as inheritance or the transfer of family names all depend on the preservation of progeny. God condemns the practice of suppressing one's legitimate progeny as well as adultery because both have a common cause: extreme greed and avarice. God says:

> Satan promises you poverty and commands you unto the offensive things, but Allah promises you forgiveness from Him and a bounty and Allah is All-encompassing, All-knowing. (The Quran, chapter *The Cow*, 2:268)

Among the offenses prompted by the fear of poverty is killing one's own children or seeking sexual pleasures without the responsibility of marriage and raising children:

> And do not kill your children out of fear of poverty. It is Us who provide for them as well as for you. Indeed killing them is a great error. And do not come near to adultery. It indeed is an act of injustice and an evil way. (The Quran, chapter *The Night Journey*, 17:31-32)

> Say, "Come. Let me relate unto you all that your Lord has forbidden unto you that you should not ascribe anything as a partner to Him and kindness to parents and that you kill not your children for fear of poverty." We provide for you and for them, "and come not close

to the offences whether what is apparent from it and what is hidden and do not kill the soul which Allah has consecrated except by the right. This is what He has admonished you unto perhaps you may understand." (The Quran, chapter *The Cattle*, 6:151)

Thus, the institution of family constitutes the most important unit of human society. If it thrives, society thrives; and if it declines, society declines as well. Society's prosperity depends on safeguarding progeny and the management of wealth. In a prophetic tradition, the Prophet, peace be upon him, is reported saying, "Bring the news of poverty and sickness to the adulterous," meaning, adultery is a cause for spreading disease and the consequent worsening of the financial conditions of the community.

CHAPTER 19

The 6ᵗʰ Principle: The Right of Society Via Equitability

This principle of wisdom is concerned with the question of equitability in its various forms: weight and measurement, the dispensation of justice, and equitability between our words (promises) and our deeds (fulfillment):

> And do not come near the property of the orphan except by way of goodness until he reaches the fullness of his strength, and fulfill the promise, for the promise is certainly going to be questioned about. And fulfill the measurement when you measure and weigh with the most upright balance. That is better and most excellent in the ultimate interpretation. (The Quran, chapter *The Night Journey*, 17:34-35)

> And do not come close to the property of the orphan except by that which is most excellent until he reaches his maturity in mind and fulfill the measurement and the weight in uprightness. We do not place a burden on any soul except that which it can bear and if you say then be just even though it be one of near of kin and fulfill Allah's promise. This is what He has admonished you unto so that perhaps you may remember. (The Quran, chapter *The Cattle*, 6:152)

Wisdom, according to its conventional definition is to put everything in its appropriate place. In other words, wisdom is to not place anything above its station or below its station. To give more than its due measure is ignorance (*jahl*), or also transgression (*'udwān*); and to give less than its due measure is wrongfulness (*ẓulm*). These are the two inherent flaws in human character that hinder one from attaining wisdom and knowledge. However, these innate disabilities can be corrected through learning and self-discipline, as God makes allowance for human shortcomings:

> And do not come close to the property of the orphan except by that which is most excellent until he reaches his maturity in mind, and fulfill the measurement and the weight in uprightness. We do not place a burden on any soul except that which it can bear, and if you speak, then be just even though it be one of near of kin, and fulfill Allah's promise. This is what He has admonished you unto so that perhaps you may remember. (The Quran, chapter *The Cattle*, 6:152)

Through the attainment of wisdom and knowledge, human beings can overcome their innate disabilities of ignorance and wrongfulness and fulfill the supreme commandment:

> Thus be as upright as you have been commanded, you and those who have turned with you [to Allah] in repentance and do not transgress, for He truly is a Seer of all that you do. And do not lean towards those who have wronged their own souls lest the fire touches you and you have no other allies besides Allah and then you will not be helped. (The Quran, chapter *Hud*, 11:112-13)

It is believed that the comment that the Prophet, peace be upon him, made about chapter *Hud* and her sister chapters was particularly highlighted in the meaning of this verse. "*Hud* and her sister chapters have made my hair gray". However, besides the commandment to "be upright," comes the gentle reminder, "Those who have turned in repentance to Allah with you." This goes to show that as many times as we keep trying to be upright but fail, we always have repentance as a recourse at our disposition. Each time we turn back to God in repentance, He makes our task lighter:

> And Allah intends to accept your repentance, but those who follow the vain desires want you to digress a great digression. Allah intends to alleviate your burden for you and the human being is created weak. (The Quran, chapter *The Women*, 4:27-28)

Even though the supreme command "be as upright" is addressed to the whole of humankind, only the repentant ones will succeed in upholding it:

> We indeed presented the trust to the heavens and the earth and

the mountains, but they refused to undertake it and they were concerned thereof, but the human being undertook it. Truly he indeed was without wisdom, without knowledge. So that Allah may punish the hypocritical men and women, and those men and women who ascribe partners to Allah and so that Allah may turn to the believer men and women and Allah is indeed Oft-Forgiving, Most Merciful. (The Quran, chapter *The Confederates*, 33:72-73)

The Dual Negations

The sixth principle is expounded through two verses in the chapter *The Night Journey*; one contains exhortations and the other a prohibition:

And do not come near the property of the orphan except by way of goodness until he reaches the fullness of his strength and fulfill the promise. For the promise is certainly going to be questioned about. And fulfill the measurement when you measure and weigh with the most upright balance. That is better and most excellent in the ultimate interpretation. (The Quran, chapter *The Night Journey*, 17:34-35)

These are exhortations to fulfill equitability in weight and management.

And do not follow that which you have no knowledge [certitude] for. Truly the hearing and the sight and the understanding, all of that are going to be questioned about. (The Quran, chapter *The Night Journey*, 17:36)

The former is a negation of wrongfulness and the latter a negation of ignorance, and these dual negations lead to a dual confirmation: wisdom and knowledge.

We indeed presented the trust to the heavens and the earth and the mountains, but they refused to undertake it and they were concerned thereof, but the human being undertook it. Truly he indeed was without wisdom, without knowledge. (The Quran, chapter *The Confederates*, 33:72)

The first step towards negating our ignorance and wrongfulness is to admit that we are ignorant and wrong. God says:

Those who keep away from the major sins and from the offences except the minor ones. Truly your Lord is abundant in the forgiveness and He knows all about you when He raised you from the earth and when you were covered in the wombs of your mothers. So do not claim yourselves to be sanctimonious. He it is who knows all about one who safeguards his soul. (The Quran, chapter *The Star*, 53:32)

O you who believe, do not follow the footsteps of Satan and whosoever follows the footsteps of Satan, he [Satan] but commands unto things which are offensive and wicked. Had it not been for Allah's favor and His mercy upon you, He would not sanctify anyone of you ever. But Allah sanctifies the one whom He pleases and Allah is All-hearing, All-knowing. (The Quran, chapter *The Light*, 24:21)

These verses lay the foundation for working towards the attainment of wisdom. By abstaining from making any claims of innocence for our soul, we make room for it to grow in wisdom; and that growth will continue to increase as long as we do not reclaim its innocence.

Similarly, with knowledge, the foundation to its growth is the realization that our souls were created without a single grain of knowledge and that all the knowledge we have was granted. By this realization, we give up any sense of entitlement to knowledge; for as long as there is something we do not know, then our knowledge cannot be complete. We must not extend our claim beyond our knowledge:

And they ask you about the spirit, say, "The spirit is from the commandment of my Lord and you are not given from the knowledge except a little." (The Quran, chapter *The Night Journey*, 17:85)

However, if we respect the boundaries of the little that we know, God may grant us more knowledge:

Far exalted is Allah, The King, The Truth, and do not be in haste with the Quran before its revelation to you is consummated, and say, "O My Lord, increase me in knowledge." (The Quran, chapter *Taha*, 20:114)

The respect for boundaries entails that we do not pronounce our view over something which we have not witnessed because that constitutes false witnessing:

> And those who do not witness the falsehood and when they pass by idle talk, they pass in a gracious manner. (The Quran, chapter *The Criterion*, 25:72)

Hence, the meaning of verse 36 in the chapter *The Night Journey*:

> And do not follow that which you have no knowledge [certitude] for. Truly the hearing and the sight and the understanding, all of that are going to be questioned about. (The Quran, chapter *The Night Journey*, 17:36)

In other words, do not employ your faculties of hearing, seeing, and understanding vainly to comprehend something which God has not allowed you to comprehend. Using them for false witnessing, constitutes abuse of their intended use. These faculties, in turn, stand as witnesses against anyone who used them abusively:

> Until when they come after it, their hearings and their sights and their skins will witness against them about all that they used to do. And they said to their skins, "Why have you witnessed against us?" They said, "Allah has made us to speak and is the One who causes everything to speak and it is He who created you the first time and unto Him you will be returned." (The Quran, chapter *Explained in Detail*, 41:20-21)

This abuse of our faculties primarily consists of passing judgment, whether affirmative or negative, without an all-encompassing knowledge:

> Nay! They claim to be a lie what they have not encompassed in knowledge, and its ultimate interpretation has not yet come unto them. Similarly, did the people before them claim [it] to be a lie. See how was the ending of those who wronged their own souls. (The Quran, chapter *Jonah*, 10:39)

> Until when they come and He says, "Did you belie My signs while you had not comprehended it in knowledge or what was it that you were doing?" (The Quran, chapter *The Ant*, 27:84)

CHAPTER 20

The 7ᵗʰ Principle: The Right of the Universe

The seventh principle is concerned with the place of human beings in the universe. It marks the beginning of a person's quest to find their station with God. In order to do so, the seeker must synchronise his pace with the universe, not overtaking it nor become overtaken by it. In order to be able to do so, he must fully express his obedience to God (*ṭaʿa*), which means to accurately respond to God whenever called upon, as the earth and the heavens did when they were called upon by God:

> Then He turned to the heaven while it was a smoke, then He said to it and to the earth, "Come both of you willingly or by compulsion." They both said, "We come willingly." (The Quran, chapter *Explained in Detail*, 41:11)

The willingness to respond whenever called is known as obedience (*ṭaʿa*). It is the expression of the total submission of one's will to the will of God. That inner state of obedience is reflected in the conduct of a person with humility and self-abandonment:

> And do not walk in the earth with conceit. Truly you will never rend the earth asunder nor will you ever tower high above the mountains. (The Quran, chapter *The Night Journey*, 17:37)

> "And take a mid-course in your walk and lower from your voice. Truly the most detestable of all sounds in the braying of the donkeys." (The Quran, chapter *Luqman*, 31:19)

And the servants of *Al-Raḥmān* are those who walk on the earth gently and when the ignorant ones address them they say, "Peace." (The Quran, chapter *The Criterion*, 25:63)

That day, they will follow the caller in whom there is no crookedness and all the voices are hushed for *Al-Raḥmān* [The All-merciful] and you will hear nothing but whispers. (The Quran, chapter *Taha*, 20:108)

And humbled will be the faces for The All-living, The Upholder of Everything and whosoever bears an offence, he indeed will meet with frustration. (The Quran, chapter *Taha*, 20:111)

In this manner, the servant of *Al-Raḥmān* continues to resonate with the universe around him until he settles down in the station designated for him in the midst of the exalted company:

By those [angels] arrayed in ranks. By those [angels] who are tugging the rope [of Allah]. By those [angels] who proclaim the remembrance [of Allah]. (The Quran, chapter *Those Ranged in Ranks*, 37:1-3)

"And there is not one among us except that for him is a station well marked. And truly we surely are those who stand in rows. And truly we surely are those who glorify Allah." (The Quran, chapter *Those Ranged in Ranks*, 37:164-166)

Establish the prayer from the setting of the sun to the darkness of the night and [establish] the prayer of dawn. Truly the prayer of the dawn is well witnessed. And in the night keep watch with it [Quran]; that is a gift of excellence for you so that perhaps your Lord may raise you to a station which is praiseworthy. (The Quran, chapter *The Night Journey*, 17:78-79)

From this point onward, it is the race to the Lord of the Throne.

PART IV

THE WISDOM OF THE SERVANTS OF AL-RAHMAN

CHAPTER 21

The Servants of Al-Raḥmān

The wisdom of the servants of *Al-Raḥmān* ('ibād *Al-Raḥmān*) consists of the same principles of wisdom of Luqman and of Muhammad, peace be upon him. In the following discussion on the points of wisdom, however, the emphasis will be on the manner in which these principles are embodied. This allows us to see these principles not merely as abstractions, but rather, as real virtues reflected and embodied by real accomplished people. It is one thing to know what is good, but entirely different to know how to do it.

For practical reasons, the usual order of the principles of wisdom has been reversed starting with the human being's synchrony with the universe and ending with the fundamental principle of God's right. The reason for this change is simple; we are here presented with accomplished people who have already assimilated all the principles and now they are living an exemplary life for the benefit of everyone.

The seven principles as embodied by the servants of *Al-Raḥmān* have been covered from verse 63 to 74 of chapter *The Criterion*. Verse 63 introduces them as people who are walking on the earth with a light:

And the servants of *Al-Raḥmān* those who walk on the earth gently and when the ignorant ones address them they say, "Peace." (The Quran, chapter *The Criterion*, 25:63)

As they walk on the earth they are in full synchrony with the rest of the universe: heavens, sun, moon, and stars. The verses immediately preceding verse 63 allude to this fact:

All blessed is He who has made in the heavens constellations of stars and has made in it a blazing lamp and a light-giving moon. And it is He who has made the night and the day to alternate for such a one who seeks to remember Allah or seeks to offer gratitude. (The Quran, chapter *The Criterion*, 25:61-62)

We are presented here with a complete cosmological panorama: the sky is above them, the earth is below them, while the sun, the moon and the constellations are in their orbits, and the night and day alternate according to their turns. They are all in sync with the servants of *Al-Raḥmān*, and the servants of *Al-Raḥmān* are in sync with them. The servants of *Al-Raḥmān* live balanced between space and time. They are neither easterly nor westerly, neither earthly nor heavenly, but in the middle of all of these in time and space. However, in order to maintain this position, they must first fulfill their duties of remembrance, gratitude, and obedience:

So acclaim Allah's glory when you are in the evening and when you are in the morning. And for Him is the praise in the heavens and in the earth and at night and when you are in the day. (The Quran, chapter *The Romans*, 30:17-18)

CHAPTER 22

The 1ˢᵗ Principle: Obedience

The first principle — existing in synchrony with the universe — is the last principle of the wisdom of Luqman and that of Prophet Muhammad, peace be upon him. It is fulfilled by answering the call of God as did the earth and the heaven:

> Then He turned to the heaven while it was a smoke then He said to it and to the earth, "Come both of you willingly or by compulsion." They both said, "We come willingly." (The Quran, chapter *Explained in Detail*, 41:11)

This willing obedience and responsiveness is expressed in the following verses:

> And the servants of *Al-Raḥmān* those who walk on the earth gently and when the ignorant ones address them they say, "Peace." And those who spend the night for their Lord prostrating and standing. (The Quran, chapter *The Criterion*, 25:63-64)

They walk gently on the earth and they speak kindly to the ignorant. Their occupation by day is to walk around the earth teaching the ignorant, warning the oblivious and spreading the word of peace. However, they pass the night in communion with *Al-Raḥmān*: in prayer, standing and prostrating, in remembrance and gratitude and obedience.

This principle pairs with verse 37 of chapter *The Night Journey* and in *Luqman* verses 18-19:

And do not walk in the earth with conceit. Truly you will never rend the earth asunder nor will you ever tower high above the mountains. (The Quran, chapter *The Night Journey*, 17:37)

And do not turn your cheek arrogantly to men and do not walk in the earth exultantly. Truly Allah does not love any self-conceited and self-vaunting. And take a mid-course in your walk and lower from your voice. Truly the most detestable of all sounds in the braying of the donkeys." (The Quran, chapter *Luqman*, 31:18-19)

CHAPTER 23

The 2ⁿᵈ Principle: Balanced Supplication

The second principle of wisdom of the servants of *Al-Rahmān* is concerned with balanced supplication. While they engage in prayer standing and prostrating, they continue to implore their Lord to grant them His mercy and save them from His chastisement:

> And those who say, "O Our Lord! Turn away from us the punishment of hell". Surely it's punishment is abasing. Truly it is woeful as a resting place [at night] and [woeful] as a station [in the day]." (The Quran, chapter *The Criterion*, 25:65-66)

A balanced prayer consists of four elements, two are regarding the content: fear and hope; and two pertain to the manner of delivery: neither with a low nor too high of a voice.

> Invoke your Lord clamorously and silently. He indeed does not love the transgressors. And do not spread corruption in the earth after that it has been set right and invoke Him out of fear and out of hope. Truly mercy of Allah is close to those who act in excellence. (The Quran, chapter *The Heights*, 7:55-56)

> Say, "Call Allah or call *Al-Rahmān*, by whichever name you call him, all the excellent names are His. And do not read your prayer aloud nor make it silent and find a way between them [neither loud nor silent]." (The Quran, chapter *The Night Journey*, 17:110)

They express their fear of the torment of the hell-fire and implore their Lord to save them from it. They balance that with the expression of hope in His mercy:

> And those who say, "O Our Lord grant unto us from our spouses and our children such as are coolness of eyes and make us leaders for those who safeguard their own souls." (The Quran, chapter *The Criterion*, 25:74)

In this manner, they make a successful prayer by mingling fear and hope with the low tone of one who is in fear and the high tone of one who is in hope. We find this exemplified in the story of Zakariah when he asked God for an heir:

> *Kaaf. Ha. Ya. 'Ain. Sad.* Mercy of your Lord remembering His slave Zakariah. When he called His Lord with a calling which was hidden. He said, "O My Lord, my bone has become feeble and my head is all ablaze with gray but never was I unfortunate in calling you O my Lord. And I indeed am concerned about my kinsfolk after me and my wife indeed is barren, therefore gift me from your presence a successor who will inherit me [in knowledge and prophethood] and inherit from the family of Jacob and make him O My Lord one that You are well pleased with." "O Zachariah! We give you glad tidings of a boy his name is Yahya. Never did We appoint any namesake for him before." (The Quran, chapter *Mary*, 19:1-7)

CHAPTER 24

The 3rd Principle: Balanced Spending

The third principle expounds one of the most fundamental tenets of wisdom: refraining from abuse and extravagance. Any type of abuse towards God's blessings is considered an act of ingratitude:

> And those who when they spend, they are neither extravagant nor miserly and they hold a middle position between them. (The Quran, chapter *The Criterion*, 25:67)

There are several verses in chapter *The Night Journey* that relate to this principle, such as the following:

> And give unto the near of kin what is due to him and unto the needy and unto the wayfarer and do not squander extravagantly. Truly the squanderers are the brethren of devils and Satan was truly ungrateful to His Lord. (The Quran, chapter *The Night Journey*, 17:26-27)

And then:

> And do not tie your hand to your neck [out of stinginess] and do not stretch it out completely or you will be sitting down blameworthy weary. Indeed your Lord expands the sustenance for whom He wills and constricts [to whom He wills]. Truly He is All-acquainted, All-seeing about His slaves. And do not kill your children out of fear of poverty. It is Us who provide for them as well as for you. Indeed killing them is a great error. (The Quran, chapter *The Night*

Journey, 17:29-31)

And fulfill the measurement when you measure and weigh with the most upright balance. That is better and most excellent in the ultimate interpretation. (The Quran, chapter *The Night Journey,* 17:35)

CHAPTER 25

The 4th Principle: The Unity of Life

The fourth principle is concerned with unity. This unity refers to three points: 1. The unity of the call to God; 2. The unity of life, and 3. The unity of man and woman through marriage.

First, all calls should be directed to one single authority, God, as this is His indivisible right. To call on anyone besides Him is a violation of His right.

Second, comes the unity of life; meaning that one life cannot be considered as distinct from another. To cause one life to live is like giving life to the entire humankind, and to take away a single life is like taking away the life of the entire humankind:

> He it is who created you from one soul and from it He made its pair so that he may find tranquility with her. So when he covered her, she carried a light burden and she went along with it. But when it got heavy, they ask Allah their Lord that if you grant us a well-formed child, surely we will be of those who offer gratitude. (The Quran, chapter *The Heights*, 7:189)

> Because of that We wrote on children of Israel that whoever kills a soul without [killing] a soul or without committing corruption in the earth it is as though he had killed the mankind altogether and anyone who gives it life [one soul] it is as though he had given life to the mankind altogether. And indeed Our messengers came unto them with clear signs but lo! Many of them after that surely became

those who went on wasting their own souls in the earth. (The Quran, chapter *The Heavenly Food Bowl*, 5:32)

Third, is the unity derived from the union which God has ordained between a man and a woman as a couple by way of matrimony. Marriage as an institution is a formal way of asking for God's permission for two souls to unite and become one. By virtue of that leave the union is attended with tranquility, mercy and affection, which is meant to produce love and contentment, mercy and healing between them. In the case of a forced union without permission, the union is attended by tension, disaffection and unfulfillment.

And among His signs is that He has created for you from yourselves mates that you may find tranquility in them and He has made between you affection and mercy. Indeed in that are signs for people who reflect. (The Quran, chapter *The Romans*, 30:21)

These three forms of unity are tightly interrelated: the unity of God cannot be fully appreciated without the unity of the soul. Only one with a united soul one can truly appreciate the one God and appreciate the meaning of His oneness. Additionally, union (through marriage) or separation of two souls, can only happen by the leave of their Creator. Manslaughter is a forced separation between two souls without the leave of the Creator, while adultery or fornication is a forced union between two souls without the leave of the Creator.

There are several verses in *The Night Journey* that highlight this relationship between killing a soul and committing adultery:

And do not come near to adultery. It indeed is an act of injustice and an evil way. And do not kill the soul which Allah has made sacred except in truth. Whoever is killed wrongfully, We have indeed given authority to His heir but let him [the heir] not exceed the limits [of just retribution; *qiṣāṣ*] in killing. For he [the heir] most certainly is helped [by Allah]. (The Quran, chapter *The Night Journey*, 17:32-33)

CHAPTER 26

The 5th Principle: Remediation

The fifth principle of wisdom concerns remediation. Considering inherent human weakness, human beings are bound to commit errors. Thus, God has provided us with the means of redeeming ourselves. This remediation procedure is known as repentance, *tawba*. It consists of three steps: 1. Belief, 2. Gratitude, and 3. Obedience. These three steps of repentance are meant to remove the three counter-effects of adultery, manslaughter or idolatry (ascribing partners to God), which are: 1. Disbelief, 2. Ingratitude, and 3. Disobedience.

> And those who do not invoke any other deity with Allah and those who do not kill the soul that Allah has made sacred except by the right and they do not commit adultery or fornication. Whoever does these, he will contract a sinful burden. And the punishment for him will be doubled on the day of resurrection and he will abide in it forever in a state of humiliation. Except such a one who turns back to Allah in repentance and reaffirms his belief and does a righteous deed. Truly it is they whose evil deeds are replaced by Allah with virtuous deeds and Allah surely is Oft-Forgiving, Most Merciful. And whoever turns back to Allah in repentance and does a righteous deed, he therefore does truly turn to Allah with a complete repentance. (The Quran, chapter *The Criterion*, 25:68-71)

1st Step: Belief

The first step in the remediation procedure is to bring one's faith back through remembrance. It is reported that the Prophet Muhammad, peace be upon him, said: "The thief doesn't steal while being a believer, the

adulterer doesn't commit adultery while being a believer" (Bukhari). Therefore, in the case where a believer forgets, he stops being a believer in that
time lapse of forgetfulness. When he returns back to remembrance, then
his faith also returns to him.

> And those who, when they commit an offensive act or otherwise
> wrong their own souls, they remember Allah and ask forgiveness
> for their sins and who forgives the sins except Allah as long as they
> do not persist knowingly on that which they have committed. (The
> Quran, chapter *The Family of Imran*, 3:135)

Remembering God translates into being aware that no one is ca-
pable of helping or saving except God. Thus, asking God for forgiveness,
istighfār, comes before repentance, *tawba*. Seeking forgiveness followed by
repentance is the means for the renewal of one's faith after it had lapsed.

2ⁿᵈ Step: Gratitude

The second step in the remediation procedure is to negate a wrong-
ful deed by a righteous deed, and an act of ingratitude by one of gratitude:

> And establish the prayer at the two ends of the day and the extrem-
> ities of the night. Lo! The good deeds expunge the bad deeds. That
> is a reminder for those who are open to remembrance. (The Quran,
> chapter *Hud*, 11:114)

> Repel the evil with that which is most excellent. We truly know that
> which they describe with their tongue. (The Quran, chapter *The Be-
> lievers*, 23:96)

In the advice given to Ibn Abbas by the Prophet, peace be upon him, comes
the following: "Follow the evil with the good, it expunges it" (Bukhari).

3ʳᵈ Step: Obedience

The third step towards complete repentance is obedience. This
works as an act of negation towards the disobedience, which was, essen-
tially turning away from God by not responding or submitting oneself to
Him. Disobedience to God consists of a discordance between the likes and
dislikes of the Master and the servant. Obedience, on the contrary, means a

complete concordance between the will and the love of the servant and His master. This concordance is obtained through the servant's relinquishing his will to the will of his Master while also giving Him the unreserved right to decide for him as He sees fit. This constitutes the essence of obedience: to accept His decision in all matters and to defer to His will.

> Say, "Nothing will ever happen to us except that which Allah has written for us. He is our master" and so let the believers put their trust in Allah. (The Quran, chapter *The Repentance*, 9:51)

With the completion of the third step, the procedure of remediation is complete, and the individual regains his or her pristine state of purity and innocence:

> Except such a one who turns back to Allah in repentance and reaffirms his belief and does a righteous deed. Truly it is they whose evil deeds are replaced by Allah with virtuous deeds and Allah surely is Oft-Forgiving, Most Merciful. (The Quran, chapter *The Criterion*, 25:70)

CHAPTER 27

The 6ᵗʰ Principle: Witnessing

A nd those who do not witness the falsehood and when they pass by idle talk, they pass in a gracious manner. (The Quran, chapter *The Criterion*, 25:72)

This principle is concerned with the difference between true witnessing and false witnessing. True witnessing consists of witnessing to what you know; and false witnessing, on the contrary, is to witness to what you do not know. In the case of the brothers of the Prophet Joseph, they said to their father Jacob:

Go back to your father and say, 'O our father! Your son has indeed committed theft and we bear witness to nothing except that which we know nor are we the guardians to the unknown. (The Quran, chapter *Joseph*, 12:81)

They meant to say that they knew as far as what the apparent evidence showed, but they could not vouch for anything that might lie beyond the apparent evidence. Therefore, their witnessing was limited to what they knew and did not extend to what they did not know which was the unseen. It is so, that while we believe in the unseen we only act on what is witnessed. This is the important correlation between the witnessed (*shahāda*) and the unwitnessed (*ghayb*). False witnessing therefore consists of claiming to witness to something you do not know because it is still within the sphere of the unwitnessed.

In chapter *The Night Journey*, the relevant verse about witnessing not only speaks about false witnessing but also about the causes that lead unto it:

> And do not follow that which you have no knowledge [certitude]
> for. Truly the hearing and the sight and the understanding, all of
> that are going to be questioned about. (The Quran, chapter *The
> Night Journey*, 17:36)

This means, do not strain your senses and your faculties in trying to witness to something which your knowledge cannot yet comprehend. Doing this constitutes a flagrant abuse of your faculties and you will be answerable for the way you use these faculties:

> And they said to their skins, "Why have you witnessed against us?"
> They said, "Allah has made us to speak and is the one who causes
> everything to speak and it is He who created you the first time and
> unto Him you will be returned." And you did not use to care to
> hide yourself lest your hearing and your sight and your skins wit-
> ness against you but you thought that Allah would not know much
> of what you used to do. (The Quran, chapter *Explained in Detail*,
> 41:21-22)

> On a day their tongues and their hands and their feet will witness
> against them for that which they used to go. (The Quran, chapter
> *The Light*, 24:24)

It is therefore bad etiquette with God to attempt to pry into the un-known — for only He knows the unknown — or even try to force your way and going ahead of Him. That is a transgression against His Grandeur. You only will know what He allows you to know, and you cannot comprehend anything of His knowledge without His permission.

> Knower of the unseen nor does He cause anyone to take a look at
> His unseen. Except such a one as He pleases from a messenger then
> He indeed will cause a guard to go ahead of him and from behind
> him. (The Quran, chapter *The Jinn*, 72:26-27)

> Allah, there is no deity except He, The All-living, The All-sustain-
> ing. Neither slumber nor sleep overtakes Him. For Him is all that
> is in the heavens and all that is in the earth. Who else can intercede
> with Him except by His leave? He knows all that is in front of them

and all that is behind them. And they do not encompass anything from His knowledge except that which He pleases. His throne encompasses the heavens and the earth and guarding the two of them does not burden Him and He is The All-High, The All-magnificent. (The Quran, chapter *The Cow*, 2:255)

He knows what is before them and what is behind them but they do not encompass Him in knowledge. (The Quran, chapter *Taha*, 20:110)

In view of these verses, the best way to get access to knowledge from God is not by straining your faculties or trying to break forcibly through the boundaries of the unseen, but rather, through patience and prayer:

O you who believe! Seek help through the patience and the prayer. Truly Allah is with those who are patient. (The Quran, chapter *The Cow*, 2:153)

If only they had patience until you had come out to them, it would have been better for them and Allah is Oft-Forgiving, Most Merciful. (The Quran, chapter *The Inner Apartments*, 49:5)

Meanwhile, until one receives knowledge about a particular matter, the safest approach is not to reject anything as false, nor accept anything as true. It is important to keep positive thinking until knowledge and certitude come and then witnessing becomes valid.

Nay! They claim to be a lie, what they have not encompassed in knowledge and its ultimate interpretation has not yet come unto them. Similarly did the people before them claimed [it] to be a lie. See how was the ending of those who wronged their own souls. (The Quran, chapter *Jonah*, 10:39)

Until when they come and He says, "Did you belie My signs while you had not comprehended it in knowledge or what was it that you were doing?" (The Quran, chapter *The Ant*, 27:84)

Therefore, it is clear that seeking more from God's knowledge is permissible as long as we take the right approach, and that right approach is gratitude (*shukr*). God says:

> And when your Lord proclaimed, "If you offer gratitude I will give you increase but if you be ungrateful surely My punishment is formidable." (The Quran, chapter *Abraham*, 14:7)

The right manner to express that gratefulness is to hold fast unto that which God has given us already in the anticipation of what is not yet given to us. As God says to Moses when Moses asked Him to see Him, God simply showed the right approach to gaining such knowledge:

> He said, "O Moses! I have indeed chosen you over mankind with My messages and with My speech. Therefore take what I have given unto you and be of those who offer gratitude." (The Quran, chapter *The Heights*, 7:144)

That gratitude, which He pointed out to Moses, was the means to His good pleasure. Once God is pleased with someone, He grants them unfettered access to His Knowledge and Mercy.

> Knower of the unseen nor does He cause anyone to take a look at His unseen. Except such a one as He pleases from a messenger then He indeed will cause a guard to go ahead of him and from behind him. (The Quran, chapter *The Jinn*, 72:26-27)

CHAPTER 28

The 7th Principle: Deliberation

And those who when they are reminded about the signs of their Lord, they do not fall upon them deaf and blind. (The Quran, chapter *The Criterion*, 25:73)

This principle teaches us about the proper way of reacting when a sign of God draws our attention or when an awareness suddenly dawns upon us. In this case we must refrain from drawing conclusions too soon. Rather, we should pause, become poised, and deliberate, exploring the various dimensions of the matter in question. We must keep away from the intrusion of our emotivity and the insinuations of our selfish self. Haste unleashes emotional onslaughts which cause the eyes to become blind and ears, deaf. Deliberation is the effective antidote against this:

> And those who when they are reminded about the signs of their Lord, they do not fall upon them deaf and blind. (The Quran, chapter *The Criterion*, 25:73)

Very often, excitement over anticipated knowledge hinders us from obtaining full comprehension of that knowledge. In such a case, until the delivery of the message is completed we must remain calm, tranquil, uneager, and content to be a spectator, rather than an actor, so that we do not obstruct the gentle flow of the divine outpour:

> Do not move your tongue with it in order to hasten with it. Indeed its gathering and recitation is upon Us. So when We have recited it, then follow its recitation. Then after it indeed it will be upon Us to explicate it. (The Quran, chapter *The Resurrection*, 75:16-19)

Far exalted is Allah, The King, The Truth and do not be in haste with the Quran before its revelation to you is consummated and say, "O My Lord, increase me in knowledge." (The Quran, chapter *Taha*, 20:114)

In a prophetic tradition, the Prophet, peace be upon him, says: "Haste is from Satan and deliberation is from Allah" (Tirmidhi).

Responding

It must be noted that haste is different from promptness. Promptness is to respond swiftly after hearing out the commandment, while haste on the contrary is to respond before fully receiving the message.

Blindness and deafness in relation to God's signs mean that His signs fall broadly into two categories: signs that are visual and others that are auditory. Remembrance can come to a person through either of the two:

> They [the disbelievers] whose eyes were in a covering from My remembrance and they were not able to hear. (The Quran, chapter *The Cave*, 18:101)

Their inability to hear the signs and rehearse them, or to see the signs and follow them is owing to the fact that their hearts are in forgetfulness and idleness:

> Truly you cannot make the dead hear and you cannot make the deaf hear the call when they turn their back away. And you are not going to guide the blind from their misguidance. You cannot make hear except one who believes in Our signs while they are in submission. (The Quran, chapter *The Ant*, 27:80-81)

> Nor are equal the living and the dead and truly Allah makes hear whom He pleases and you are not going to be able to make them hear those that are in the graves. (The Quran, chapter *The Originator*, 35:22)

Those who turn their back in disbelief and those who lay in their graves are all equal, they are all dead. The living person in the sight of God is one who has faith and the dead person is the one who is without faith.

As the dead cannot respond to the signs of God when reminded, so is the disbeliever who doesn't respond when reminded. The deaf cannot respond; the dead cannot respond. In a similar manner, when the dead are reminded through a visual sign they cannot see it, so too are the non-submitters who cannot see the signs of God when reminded through them because they are blind.

Conversely, those who have faith in their hearts, when reminded through an auditory sign of God, hear it, process it, and understand it. Those who have submitted (*taslīm*) to God, when reminded by a visual sign they see it and ascertain it. Therefore, the believers and the submitters, when reminded by the signs of their Lord, do not fall upon them deaf and blind. On the contrary, they hear them and understand the messages or they see them and gain certitude about their true meaning. After understanding and ascertaining, they proceed to act upon them:

> Say, "Look and see that which is in the heavens and in the earth" But signs [of glad tidings] and warnings will avail not a people who do not believe. (The Quran, chapter *Jonah*, 10:101)

Channels of Processing

The channels of processing for those who are reminded through auditory signs and are distinct from those who are reminded through visual signs. One channel is the "understanding process" (*'aql*) and the other is the "ascertaining process" (*istiqān/yaqīn*).

The *understanding* channel starts from faith (*īmān*), to remembrance (*dhikr*), to reflection (*fikr*), to hearing (*sama'*) and then understanding (*'aql*). As for the *ascertaining* channel, it starts from self-submission (*islām*), to remembrance, to reflection, to watching (*naẓar*) and then to seeing (*baṣar*) or ascertaining (*istiqān*). Remembrance (*dhikr*) and reflection (*fikr*) are common to both channels. (See diagram)

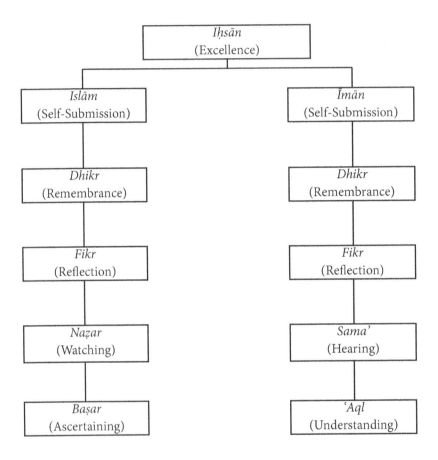

CONCLUSION

In conclusion, I feel obliged to remind the reader that merely absorbing the content of this book intellectually in no way means that they have elevated to the noble rank of the wise ones. Wisdom, above all, is a divinely given bounty:

> He gives the wisdom unto whom He pleases and whosoever the wisdom is given to, he indeed is given a lot of good but none does remember except the people of the living heart. (The Quran, chapter *The Cow*, 2:269)

Those who are selected to receive this most magnificent prize have only one common merit: positiveness (*ḥusn al ẓann*). This means that they have an unshakable faith in the power of good and in the goodness of God.

> And the good and the evil are not equal. Push back [evil] with that which is most excellent and one between you and him there is an enmity, lo! It is as though he is an ally and an intimate friend. (The Quran, chapter *Explained in Detail*, 41:34)

> Repel the evil with that which is most excellent. We truly know that which they describe with their tongue. (The Quran, chapter *The Believers*, 23:96)

The distinctive mark of those who think well of Him is that willingness to give unto Him whatever they are asked to give. This willingness to surrender is the critical mark of positiveness. It marks the first step towards establishing a bond of love between human beings and God. God gave first and then asks us to give back so that the giving and taking can continue for eternity. There are those who received and then didn't feel right to give back but there are those who willingly gave back — and they continued to take and then give. And these are the ones who merit to have wisdom:

Is the reward for excellence any other than the excellence? (The Quran, chapter *The All-Merciful*, 55:60)

Wisdom is one of those rewards given back to those who show their willingness to do good like Joseph and Moses in the following verses:

And when he reached the age of maturity, We gave him wisdom and knowledge. Thus do We reward those who act in excellence. (The Quran, chapter *Joseph*, 12:22)

And when he reached the fullness of his strength and reached complete maturity of mind, We gave him wisdom and knowledge and it is thus that We reward those who act in excellence. (The Quran, chapter *The Stories*, 28:14)

They were given wisdom for the goodness that God saw in their hearts. But once given, God will soon try the one unto whom He gave in order to see whether they still maintain the positive attitude they had before they acquired wisdom. That trial is about whether we will be grateful and be given more, or be ungrateful.

And We indeed gave the wisdom unto Luqman saying, "Now do offer gratitude to Allah." Thus whosoever offers gratitude [to Allah], he only thus offers gratitude for the good of his own soul and whoever is ungrateful, truly Allah is All-self-sufficient, All- worthy of praise. (The Quran, chapter *Luqman*, 31:12)

In a similar manner, both Joseph and Moses were tried right after they were given wisdom to see if they would be grateful or not. As for Joseph, he was tried with the supernatural beauty that God had given him to see whether he would use it abusively by yielding to the seductive invitation of the wife of his master and thereby cheat God, his master and himself, or whether he would stand up for God and deny the temptation in recognition of the goodness God granted to him and his master.

But she in whose house he was, sought to prevail with him [in order to seduce him] and she fastened the doors and said, "I am ready for you." He said, "God forbid. He is indeed my Lord who made my sojourn an excellent one. Truly, those who wrong their own souls do not prosper." And she was indeed enamoured by him and he was solicitous on her account had it not been for the proof which he saw from his Lord. So that We turn away from him the evil and the injustice. For truly he was from among Our selected slaves. And they both raced to the door and she tore his shirt from behind and they both found her master [husband] at the door. She said, "What is the reward of someone who harbors evil at your family if not imprisonment or a painful punishment." He said, "It was she who sought to prevail with me over myself" and a witness witnessed from her own folk, "If his shirt was torn from the front, then she is right and it is he who is of the liars. But if his shirt is torn from the back, then she lied and it is he who is among the truthful." So when he saw his shirt torn from behind he said, "It is from your scheming (womenfolk). Your scheming is indeed awesome." O Joseph! Let this pass and you (O wife) seek forgiveness for your sin. For you indeed are of those who were in error." (The Quran, chapter *Joseph*, 12:23-29)

Joseph remained grateful and abandoned his pleasure for the pleasure of his Lord.

Like Joseph, Moses was also tried right after receiving wisdom from God although the trial was of a different kind:

And when he reached the fullness of his strength and reached complete maturity of mind, We gave him wisdom and knowledge and it is thus that We reward those who act in excellence. And he entered the city at a time when its people were off their guard and he found therein two men fighting, this one from his own faction and this one from his enemies, and the one from his faction called out to him for help against the one who is from his enemy, so Moses struck him with his fist and thus he killed him and he said, "This is of the work of Satan. He truly is an enemy who clearly leads people astray. He said, "O My Lord! I have indeed wronged my own soul therefore forgive me" so He forgave him, for He indeed is He who is The Oft-Forgiving, The Most Merciful. He said, "O My Lord! Since that you have blessed me therefore I shall never be a supporter for the evildoers." And he spent the night in the city until morning fearful and was vigilant and behold the one who sought his help yesterday is again crying out to him for help. Then Moses said to him, "You indeed are truly in open error." But when he wanted to lay hands on the one who was an enemy to both of them he [the Israelite] said, "O Moses, do you want to kill me as you killed a soul yesterday? You want to be but a tyrant in the land and you do not want to be of those who make things right." (The Quran, chapter *The Stories*, 28:14-19)

In the case of Moses, he was tried in the matter of the supernatural strength that God had given him, to see whether he would use this strength abusively or use it to help the weak and the oppressed.

As we see, God tried both of these prophets after He had given them wisdom. Joseph was tried with the temptation of the flesh which draws a person nearer to adultery. Moses on his part was tried through the temptation of blood because a person of his blood relation appealed to him against an outsider; the Israelite against the Egyptian. That intervention lead to an unintended excessive use of force leading to the death of the Egyptian. For this Moses asked forgiveness from his Lord and it was granted. This man picked a fight with another Egyptian and again begged for help from Moses. Moses first chided him for his pugnacity and then proceed to intervene, but God warned him on the tongue of the very Israelite he was intending to help. Had he intervened a second time that would have been akin to taking the lives of two souls in defense of one soul. He was justified (and forgiven) in the previous circumstance because his actions fell into the principle of "life for life."

The temptation of the flesh and the urges of the blood are some of the major obstacles to the attainment of wisdom for they lead to two of the most serious offenses: adultery and murder.

And those who do not invoke any other deity with Allah and those who do not kill the soul that Allah has made sacred except by the right and they do not commit adultery or fornication. Whoever does these, he will contract a sinful burden. (The Quran, chapter *The Criterion*, 25:68)

And do not come near to adultery. It indeed is an act of injustice and an evil way. And do not kill the soul which Allah has made sacred except in truth. Whoever is killed wrongfully, We have indeed given authority to His heir but let him [the heir] not exceed the limits [of just retribution; *qiṣāṣ*] in killing. For He [the heir] most certainly is helped [by Allah]. (The Quran, chapter *The Night Journey*, 17:32-33)

These examples demonstrate that anyone who is given wisdom will be tried along the two most common trials: the trial through flesh and the trial through blood. Once they succeed after these trials, then, their word becomes just and their soul justified.

INDEX

A

Aaron 14, 23
Abraham 12, 14, 29, 35, 64
Abu Hurayra 55
Abu Sa'eed al Khudri 49
Abu Talib 56
Abyssinia 28
adultery 75, 76, 77, 95, 96, 110
Ahmad 55
'Ali 11
al sālik al mujāwib. See true traveller
al sālik al mutlaq. See perrenial traveller
Aminah 11
'aql 45, 105
'aql al akbar. See the supreme intellect
ascertaining channel 105
asrār 54
attributes (of God) 8, 9
'azamah 62

B

basar 105
Bayhaqi 50
birr al wālidayn 65
Bukhari 2, 5, 20, 44, 45, 52, 55, 56, 97
Burāq 49

C

Christianity 28
criterion 13, 14

D

David 34, 35, 42

dā'ī 25
Dawud. *See* David
dhikr 37, 42, 105
 dhikr al akbar 37

E

essence (of God) 8, 9

F

faculties 82, 100, 101
Fatimah 11
fikr. See reflection
fitra 45, 49, 52
furqān 13

G

Gabriel 44, 45, 49, 50, 52
ghinā 40
good pleasure of God 66, 67, 102

H

Ḥadīth Qudsiy 9, 36
hamd 40
haqq 4, 22
haqq al taqwa 62
Haroon. *See* Aaron
hayba 51
hearing 3, 36, 104, 105
hikma 1, 42
 al hikma al 'uliyā 4
 hikma al dāba 1
 hikmat 4
horizontal 1, 45, 46
 horizontal journey 50, 52, 55

Made in the USA
Monee, IL
29 January 2024